The Servant's Heart

By

Dr. Clare R. Ernstzen

" The Servant's Heart"

© 2013 Clare R Ernstzen

First Edition First Impression 2013

Printed by Hebron Press

P O Box 11118, Rynfield, 1514, RSA

ISBN 978-1-868462-63-6

Dr. CLARE ERNSTZEN

Acknowledgements

With thanks to Nicole Erdis for editing this book

PREFACE

Let me begin by saying the reason I chose the particular title, "The Servant's Heart", was as a result of my own experiences. When changes in my life started taking place, I was not aware of what was being accomplished, or where these changes would take me.

At the time, a friend happened to mention the term 'A Servant's Heart', and this led me to the realisation of what was happening to my life. During this season I became aware of the reality that, whilst many of the attributes of the servant's heart are common knowledge, there seemed to be no comprehensive teaching. Insight into the various attributes of servanthood; those to be abolished, those to be acquired, and the significance of each trial that would be associated with this change of heart.

The scope for research on this topic is endless as the generic term "The Servant's Heart" is not necessarily well understood.

The purpose of this book is to promote a wider understanding of the concept "servant's heart"; to encourage believers; and to provide a barometer which the Holy Spirit can use to prompt believers regarding what to be aware of.

Unless believers undergo this kind of heart change, their lives will remain unaltered, and their hearts hardened. They may need to endure rebuke for the hardness of their hearts, as did the disciples in Mark 16:14.

[14] Later He appeared to the eleven as they sat at the table; and He rebuked their unbelief and hardness of heart, because they did not believe those who had seen Him after He had risen.[1]

Would we not all rather hear the words, "Well done good and faithful servant"?

Author

Dr. CLARE ERNSTZEN

Table Of Contents

Preface 4
Table Of Contents 5
Introduction 6
Chapter 1
What are the characteristics of a servant's heart? 11
Chapter 2
What characteristics should a servant's heart be without? 39
Chapter 3
Why do we need a servant's heart? 61
Chaper 4
How do we receive a servant's heart? 64
Chapter 5
What is the current trend of today's Christian with regards to the necessity of a servant's heart? 71
Chapter 6
Biblical examples of people with servant's hearts? 74
Chaper 7
Characters in the Bible that refused the change of heart offered to them by the Lord 90
Chapter 8
What are the practical component's of a servant's heart? 93
Chapter 9
Servant Leadership 100
Chapter 10
Intercession and the servant's heart 139
Chapter 11
Biblical examples of Servant Leadership 144
Conclusion 155
Bibliography 156

Introduction

Jesus taught that the greatest in the Kingdom of God is the least. In this study we will look at the practical aspects of this teaching, and how it epitomises the ministry of Jesus Christ and other Biblical characters. How can our hearts be changed to that of a servant's?

So, what is the definition of a servant and what do the Scriptures say about this?

Nelson's New Christian Dictionary has this definition of a servant:
> **Servant:** Status of a leader. Christ fulfilled the role of a suffering servant. Luther described Christians as the servants of all (Matt. 20:27; Mark 10:42–45; 2 Cor. 4:5). [2]

Matthew 23:11,
> [11] But he who is greatest among you shall be your servant.[3]

Isaiah 42:1-4
> "Behold! My Servant whom I uphold,
> My Elect One *in whom* My soul delights!
> I have put My Spirit upon Him;
> He will bring forth justice to the Gentiles.
> [2] He will not cry out, nor raise *His voice,*
> Nor cause His voice to be heard in the street.
> [3] A bruised reed He will not break,
> And smoking flax He will not quench;
> He will bring forth justice for truth.
> [4] He will not fail nor be discouraged,
> Till He has established justice in the earth;
> And the coastlands shall wait for His law."[4]

Isaiah 49:1-6
> "Listen, O coastlands, to Me,
> And take heed, you peoples from afar!
> The Lord has called Me from the womb;
> From the matrix of My mother He has made mention of My name.
>
> [2] And He has made My mouth like a sharp sword;
> In the shadow of His hand He has hidden Me,
> And made Me a polished shaft;
> In His quiver He has hidden Me."
>
> [3] "And He said to me,
> 'You *are* My servant, O Israel,
> In whom I will be glorified.'
>
> [4] Then I said, 'I have labored in vain,
> I have spent my strength for nothing and in vain;
> Yet surely my just reward *is* with the Lord,
> And my work with my God.' "
>
> [5] "And now the Lord says,

> Who formed Me from the womb *to be* His Servant,
> To bring Jacob back to Him,
> So that Israel is gathered to Him
> (For I shall be glorious in the eyes of the Lord,
> And My God shall be My strength),
>
> [6] Indeed He says,
> 'It is too small a thing that You should be My Servant
> To raise up the tribes of Jacob,
> And to restore the preserved ones of Israel;
> I will also give You as a light to the Gentiles,
> That You should be My salvation to the ends of the earth.' "[5]

Isaiah 50:4-9,
> [4] "The Lord God has given Me
> The tongue of the learned,
> That I should know how to speak
> A word in season to *him who is* weary.
> He awakens Me morning by morning,
> He awakens My ear
> To hear as the learned.
> [5] The Lord God has opened My ear;
> And I was not rebellious,
> Nor did I turn away.
> [6] I gave My back to those who struck *Me*,
> And My cheeks to those who plucked out the beard;
> I did not hide My face from shame and spitting.
>
> [7] "For the Lord God will help Me;
> Therefore I will not be disgraced;
> Therefore I have set My face like a flint,
> And I know that I will not be ashamed.
>
> [8] *He is* near who justifies Me;
> Who will contend with Me?
> Let us stand together.
> Who *is* My adversary?
> Let him come near Me.
>
> [9] Surely the Lord God will help Me;
> Who *is he who* will condemn Me?
> Indeed they will all grow old like a garment;
> The moth will eat them up.[6]

Have you ever wondered what made Jesus' ministry different from any other, apart from the fact that He was the Son of God? Jesus became angry, tired, hungry and thristy, like us, but what made His ministry so spectacular? What made

Jesus willing to feed the multitudes that followed Him so much that He had to "steal" quiet time by 'disappearing' in the early mornings?

What was Jesus illustrating when He washed the disciples' feet? (John 13). How did Jesus manage to have compassion and love for everybody? How did He maintain that air of gentleness that we see pictured in the Gospels, but still have the authority to tell the storm to calm? (Luke 8).

Why did Jesus tell so many parables about people serving others? There is the parable of the Good Samaritan (Luke 10), that of the good shepherd (Matthew 18), and the parable of the servants given talents by their master (Luke 19)? Surely Jesus was encouraging us to serve each other, to serve God, and to realise that we need to live harmoniously?

We could ask why is it so difficult today to find the grace to thank a parking attendant. To find a waitress that has your interests at heart – (after all you are the customer). To find someone at the other side of a service desk with a smile and a willing-to-serve attitude (rather than a bored, arrogant, listless demanding one).

What about your own heart? Would you be prepared to fetch and carry for someone less fortunate than yourself? Are you prepared to spend time and effort for someone who is not able to repay you with anything other than a smile and the words "thank you"? Would you submit in the same manner to someone above you? What is your attitude to those in authority, or do you resent their instructions? (1 Timothy 2:1-2 and Romans 13:1-7)

Are you appreciative of your salvation, or is it the same as your Passport? In the cupboard, kept up to date for emergencies, but never really used, and certainly not thought about everyday.

If following Jesus today meant walking from place to place come rain, sunshine or hail, hot or cold; feeling constantly dusty and sweaty; being greeted by maniacal Pharisees wanting to throw you off a cliff; having to physically catch your dinner in the lake; standing in the hot sun with ten to fifteen thousand people milling around; and listening to a speaker without the effects of a Public Address system - Have you ever thought about that miracle? Fifteen thousand men, women and screaming children listening to one man's voice on the top of a mountain without an amplifier? Would that appeal to you? Or would your twenty-first-century heart need a transplant before you would lower yourself to becoming a follower of Jesus?

A servant's heart, in a nutshell, is a heart that beats for others. It desires to see the Lord glorified in everything; longs to wash the Lord's feet; to spend a years salary on perfume and pour it out on His feet; a heart that desires above all else to be one with the heart like Jesus. It is a heart that has prostrated itself before the throne of God and humbly waits for instructions from the Master. A heart

Dr. CLARE ERNSTZEN

that desires nothing more than to follow where the Holy Spirit leads; a heart that is content to be whatever Jesus desires it to be, whether serving people, serving Jesus, or serving the Holy Spirit.

CHAPTER 1
What Are The Characteristics Of A Servant's Heart?

A Servant's Heart is demonstrated by the personality of the person in at least the following ways:

- Love
- Compassion
- Humility / Meekness
- Longsuffering
- Peace

Let us now look at these characteristics and see how they are demonstrated in the lives of every believer who opens his heart to the working of the Holy Spirit.

LOVE

Brian Bailey, in his book "The Comforter", defines Love – one of the fruits of the Spirit, as the following:

> The definition of love is commitment. Love is not based on feelings, although feelings do flow as the fruit of love matures. Therefore love starts in the will, or in the spirit, and then flows to the soul, the area of our emotions. Finally, it is expressed by the outward actions, such as acts of touching and kindness.[7]

We have various examples of how God shows His love towards us. There are several Scriptures that confirm the love of God for us, including the lengths to which this love will extend.

John 3:16,
[16] For God so loved the world that He gave His only begotten Son, that whoever believes in Him should not perish but have everlasting life. [8]

Jeremiah 31:3,
[3] The Lord has appeared of old to me, saying:"Yes, I have loved you with an everlasting love; Therefore with lovingkindness I have drawn you.[9]

Romans 5:8
[8] But God demonstrates His own love toward us, in that while

we were still sinners, Christ died for us.[10]

John 15:13
¹³ Greater love has no one than this, than to lay down one's life for his friends.[11]

What Jesus Christ is saying is in the above statement, is that such a person will willingly give up his own life for the benefit of the someone else; he is willing to be a 'sacrifice' - to be the scapegoat - for the punishment deserved by another person. This was Jesus' actions to save us.

Laying down our life in love can also be done figuratively. We have the option of 'laying down our lives' by adopting and showing the attitudes of Christ towards others. Self-preservation, or protecting our reputation, often becomes a stumbling block in our lives. We should remember that on earth Jesus did not attempt to protect his reputation.

Philippians 2:6-11
⁶ who, being in the form of God, did not consider it robbery to be equal with God, ⁷ but made Himself of no reputation, taking the form of a bondservant, *and* coming in the likeness of men. ⁸ And being found in appearance as a man, He humbled Himself and became obedient to *the point of* death, even the death of the cross. ⁹ Therefore God also has highly exalted Him and given Him the name which is above every name, ¹⁰ that at the name of Jesus every knee should bow, of those in heaven, and of those on earth, and of those under the earth, ¹¹ and *that* every tongue should confess that Jesus Christ *is* Lord, to the glory of God the Father.[12]

Jesus was willing to give up His life, position, status and reputation to embrace a symbol of a curse because of His love for us. According to the Law, anyone hanged on a tree was accursed. (Deuteronomy 21:23) Jesus became a curse to set us free from the curse of sin. Because Jesus was willing to lay down His life for us, God exalted Him to the highest place possible. This epitomises one of the hardest attributes of the servant's heart - the ability to lose everything so that someone else will gain.

When the fifth-century bishop of Constantinople, Chrysostom, was driven from the city into exile, he wrote a friend, "When I was driven from the city, I felt no anxiety, but said to myself, "If the empress wishes to banish me, let her do so; the earth is the Lord's. If she wants to have me sawn asunder, I have Isaiah for an example. If she wants me to be drowned in the ocean, I think of Jonah. If I am to be thrown into the fire, the three men in the furnace suffered the same. If cast before wild beasts, I remember Daniel in the lions' den. If she wants me to be stoned, I have before me Stephen, the first martyr. If she demands my head, let her do so; John the Baptist shines before me. Naked I came from my mother's womb; naked shall I leave this world."[13]

Laying down our lives figuratively is also linked with the idea of us not taking offences at other people's actions, mannerisms or behaviour patterns. This brings us to the subject of dying to self and living for Christ. Nobody can harm a dead person. If we really are dead to the world, then we will not react and become defensive and angry when we are not treated well. Human pride takes offence, but a humble spirit cannot be offended.

Dying to self means irrevocable commitment to the glory of God. This involves the removal of all comfort zones as the Lord leads into areas that are particularly sensitive. Dying to self means: to choose Christ's will instead of our own personal preferences, reputation, thoughts, desires, ambitions or abilities.

"There came a day when George Mueller died, utterly died! No longer did his own desires, preferences, and tastes come first. He knew that from then on Christ must be all in all. George Mueller, when asked the secret of his victorious Christian life.[14]

As a result of this experience your entire being will re-focus on the Lord, His Return and His Salvation, His love for the lost and His compassion and grace. There will be nothing of more importance than this in your life. The level to which you are prepared to hand over your life to the Lord will be the measure of your death experience with Christ.

We have probably all heard the term for the God kind of love - *agape*. The meaning of this is really the kind of love that does not do what the loved one desires, but rather does what the one who loves deems necessary. This puts a totally different outlook on God's love for us. 1 Corinthians Chapter 13 lists a few examples of this love:

Love :-
   Endures long.
Literally, in every sense of the word, love endures forever. It does not keep a record of things suffered, nor give up when the going gets rough, but continues unwaveringly.

   Is patient.
Patience is added to endurance. Again, this is love no matter what happens or how long the person takes to change.

   Is kind.
In kindness, graciously accepting those who have fallen; reaffirming Christian love, without recrimination or slight.

   Never jealous or envious.
When someone shows spiritual growth, is victorious over sin, or perhaps receives spiritual understanding by the Holy Spirit, love will not permit jealousy but will rejoice with that person.

> Never boastful or haughty.

Love does not permit us to boast about anything except the Lord.

> Not conceited.

Love does not allow us to think more highly about ourselves than we should.

> Not rude.

Love is polite and gentle.

> Does not insist on its own rights or ways.

Love is not self-assertive but allows the Holy Spirit to lead in all things.

> Not self-seeking.

Love ensures that others are not given preference, and insists that Jesus Christ must receive all the praise, honour and glory.

> Not touchy, fretful or resentful.

Love gives glory to God, and not to self. It sees God in control of all events, even if they seem to be going the wrong way.

> Pays no attention to a suffered wrong.

Love does not dwell on past hurts but forgives unconditionally.

> Does not rejoice at injustice or at unrighteousness.

Love never wants to get even, nor does it permit acts that will cause disgrace to the Name of Jesus.

> Bears up under everything and anything.

Love understands from where attacks come, and considers them as instruments to transform character into the image of Christ.

> Believes the best in each person.

Love sees people as God does - the finished person. Love sees people through the eyes of faith as to what they will attain.

> Hopes unfading in all circumstances.

Love never gives up on a situation.

> Endures without weakening.

Love remains steadfast no matter what the circumstances look like right.

> Never fails.

No matter what, love still loves with no regrets, boundaries or inhibitions. Love is an eternal quality.

This list in itself is enough to make most of us realise the hardness of our own character and heart. If someone was to behave in a manner towards you which degraded your reputation, and you exhibited the above qualities, you would be labelled a "doormat" by those who do not have the mind of Christ. God's eyes roam the earth seeking those on whose behalf He can show Himself strong. (2 Chronicles 16:9). We must learn to rest in the unshakeable peace of the Lord, and trust in Him for righteousness to prevail.

COMPASSION

The Oxford Dictionary defines compassion as being pity that inclines one to be helpful or merciful.

There are different examples of compassion in the Bible, and we will look at some of them.

God's Compassion:-
Exodus 3:7-8,

⁷ And the Lord said: "I have surely seen the oppression of My people who *are* in Egypt, and have heard their cry because of their taskmasters, for I know their sorrows. ⁸ So I have come down to deliver them out of the hand of the Egyptians, and to bring them up from that land to a good and large land, to a land flowing with milk and honey, to the place of the Canaanites and the Hittites and the Amorites and the Perizzites and the Hivites and the Jebusites. [15]

God's kind of compassion (at work here) shows that He had heard their cries of affliction, had decided to take them out of their affliction, but it would involve a long walk, hardships and war to remove those who illegally possessed the land God had declared was theirs.

Have you you taken the long walk towards obtaining a servant's heart, or are you remaining under the oppression of the 'taskmasters'?

God shows His compassion in many other ways in the Bible. God had compassion on us in that while we were yet sinners, Christ died for us (Romans 5:8). God abhors sin, but because He loves us so much, He made a way for us to receive forgiveness for our sins, even though we were so deep in sin that He could not look at us.

Compassion means to have pity in a way that motivates us to be helpful. This cost God the life of His Son.

God spent many years permitting sin to be covered (atonement), and He became weary of sacrifices of rams, goats and bulls. He wanted companionship from those He had created. He longed for fellowship with those with broken spirits and contrite hearts (Psalm 51:16-17).

Jesus Christ's Compassion:-
We will now look into the various aspects of the compassion that Jesus Christ showed and His responses to the circumstances that aroused His compassion.

Jesus' ability to do something when His compassion was aroused.

What made Jesus different from those around Him was that when His compassion was aroused He had the miraculous ability to change the circumstances.

Why did Jesus have the power of God released in His life, and what is preventing us from experiencing the release of that same power in our lives?

God is searching for those who are consistent; that follow after His heart the same way David did, the same way Jesus did (1 Samuel 13:14). They were both consistent in serving God. Jesus stated that He did nothing that He had not heard the Father command. (this was not blindly blundering on; hoping that eberything would turn out right by quoting Romans 8:28.)
Another reason for the lack of power today is the apathy of so-called Christians towards God Himself. How many people really want to see God's power, and actually believe that this power is available for today? Consider the teaching of Jesus on '... whatsoever you ask in My name, believing, you will receive' (John 14:13,14), how many people today pray believing that they will receive God's answer? Are not most prayers a result of fear? If a sick person trult believed that God would heal, would that person not be thankful in advance, knowing that as they asked, the healing was already given?

When Jesus prayed for someone, He knew beyond a shadow of a doubt that His father, God, was willing and able to heal the person, that restoration would follow because that is the heart of God. Jesus never prayed for someone with a fear that the person might not be acceptable to God the Father. (John 11:41-42) Jesus knew Father intimately. He knew that He should thank the Father because, as He prayed, God's power was released through Him.

Jesus knew that in His humanity there was nothing that He could do to heal the sick, raise the dead, or achieve anything else (John 5:19-20). Jesus exhibited the servant's heart with the knowledge that all power came from the Father, God. Jesus was totally dependent upon His heavenly father.

Jesus fed the hungry on various occasions.
Throughout the Gospels there are references to Jesus' feeding of the multitudes. Jesus understood that these people had need of physical food as well as spiritual food, and He supplied both. Jesus knew about human limitations.

We have various references to Jesus healing all the sick that came to Him.
The Gospels all relate the various incidents of healing performed by Jesus. Amongst all the examples, we have a few occasions where the Gospel writers simply state that Jesus healed all the sick among them. This kind of compassion was evident in Jesus' every action. We know that in Acts 10:38, Peter spoke of how Jesus went about healing all those who were sick and were oppressed of the devil. Jesus knew that the cause of sickness was satan oppression. Knowing this, He was able to show compassion.

As our eyes are opened to spiritual things, God allows us to see the demonic forces at work. This insight gives us the ability to separate the oppression from the person. We need this revelation from God because then we are able to understand the real source of sin, and to see the soul as God sees it. Satan continues to rules this world for a while because of Adam's sin, but this does not stop God from loving every soul He created, as we see in Psalm 139.

Jesus wept at Lazarus' grave. (John 11:35)
Dutch sheets gives wonderful insight into the principles of intercessory prayer, in his book titles "Intercessory Prayer".

"According to these verses the tears Christ shed were not merely tears of sympathy, but of indignation and the stirrings of His spirit. We also know that they were taking place in the context of prayer because verse 41 informs us that before raising Lazarus from the dead, Jesus said to the Father, "I thank Thee that Thou heardest Me." He then gave the command, "Lazarus, come forth."[16]

Compassion comes in many forms and ways, and intercessory prayer will be one of the ways we are used as instruments of the Lord. This type of prayer is when we intercede on behalf of another because of the burden placed in our spirits by the Holy Spirit.

"According to Webster, intercede means "to go or pass between;
to act between parties with a view to reconcile those who differ
or contend; to interpose; to mediate or make intercession; mediation,"

Using the same source, mediate means "between two extremes; to interpose between parties as the equal friend of each; to negotiate between persons at variance with a view to reconciliation; to mediate a peace; intercession."

Please notice that these terms are largely synonymous with some of the same words used to define each - between, interpose and reconcile. Notice also that one is used to define the other: mediation defines intercession and intercession defines mediation.

As can be clearly seen from these definitions, the concept of intercession can be summarised as mediating, going between, pleading for another, representing one party to another for, but not limited to, legal situations.

Intercession happens in our courts daily with lawyers interceding for clients.

Intercession happens in contractual meetings daily with attorneys representing one party to another.

Intercession happens in offices and business meetings daily as secretaries or other associates "go between", representing one to another. Nothing spiritual about it.

It involves delegation.

It involves authority.

It boils down to representation. As we discussed in the previous chapter, to represent means to re-present, or present again." [17]

With a basic understanding of intercessory prayer we can understand what we are doing when we present a person or situation before the throne of God.

1 Timothy 2:5
⁵ For there is one God and one mediator between God and mankind, the man Christ Jesus, [18]

This means that Jesus Christ intercededs or mediates for each one of us before the Throne of Grace, so that we can be clothed in Jesus Christ's righteousness and approach the Throne of Grace boldly in a time of need. (Hebrews 4:16)

Therefore, when we intercede, we know our prayers are heard. This is because we stand in the righteousness of Jesus Christ, and because Jesus Christ Himself mediates with the Father on our behalf that our prayers are heard and accepted. With this change of thinking we no longer approach the Father in fear because we know we are accepted by the Father.

Knowig this, the heats attitude of a servant becomes very effective as an instrument of compassion in intercessory prayer.

Jesus understood the cost of the offering of the widow who put in the two mites (Mark 12)
When Jesus was at the Temple with His disciples, watching the woman bring her offering of two mites, He commented that the woman had given far more than any of the other people who had placed an offering from their riches. When we give our hearts and lives as the offering, we too place far more in the hands of our Saviour than those people who give from their financial resources, but never let their hearts be warmed by His love.

Something we fail to realise is that it is God who gives us the power to gain wealth. He already owns the cattle on a thousand hills. Why then would He even want our finances?

Deuteronomy 8:18
⁸ "And you shall remember the Lord your God, for *it is* He who gives you power to get wealth, that He may establish His covenant which He swore to your fathers,

as *it is* this day.[19]

When we give our lives as the Levites did, we offer up the very most we can give - ourselves. Our greatest offering is the sacrifice of our volition so that He can use us. We, too, put our two mites into the hands of the owner of the universe, and stand amazed as God uses them to build His Church.

When we come to the Father and offer Him ourselves, He releases the floodgates of Heaven, and show himself strong on our behalf. There is nothing that can hinder the work of the Lord more than those individuals who resents loosing first place for themselves. Hearts that are freely relinquished to the Father's will are the greatest asset in the Kingdom of God.

When we stand before the Father, and genuinely offer our lives to Him, we know that Jesus Christ Himself understands the cost we are prepared to pay for the relationship we desire. Jesus knew the cost that dying for us would involve, and He was willing to pay that price. We, too, should be prepared to pay the price so that others might see Christ forms in us and yearn for the love of the Saviour..

Compassion and the Servant's Heart
The servant's heart in us is moved by compassion as the love of God for others flows through our lives. We are made aware by the Holy Spirit of what God feels and sees in human situations. While God will not necessarily remove adverse circumstances from our lives – especially those we have begun by our own error - He will stand with us as we reap what we have sown. He will not judge us after we have repented.

The servant's heart will be inclined to help in the circumstances seen around them, and endeavour to bring people closer to God in whatever way possible. This at times will involve personal cost.

There is another word associated with compassion, and that is tenderness. This can involve our treatment of others, but it should also be an attribute of our hearts. Tenderness is the ability to allow the Lord to let us feel what others are feeling. This availability on our behalf means we submit to allowing our hearts to experience the anguish another is suffering. This is one way the Holy Spirit can guide and lead us in ministry to others.

This tenderness also means we are soft to the workings of the Lord in our own hearts. It causes us to respond quickly gentle rebukes from the Lord with regards to our personal lives.

Such tenderness is demonstrated in mercy, but is also seen when a person is so tender they are moved with emotion for the slightest demonstration of God's Love and favour.

Humility and Meekness

Dr. CLARE ERNSTZEN

Humility is a vital key in the servant's hearts attitude. We cannot find our true position in Christ until such time as we understand the meaning of humility - what it is, and what it is not.

"The faithful servant who recognises his position finds a real pleasure in supplying the wants of the master or his guests. When we see that humility is something infinitely deeper than contrition, and accept it as our participation in the life of Jesus, we will begin to learn that is our true nobility. We will begin to understand that being servants of all is the highest fulfilment of our destiny, as men created in the image of God." (Humility, Andrew Murray, pg 7.)[20]

"The accusation that those who claim to be seeking the higher holiness have not always done so with increased humility is a call to all earnest Christians to prove that meekness and lowliness of heart are the chief marks by which they follow the meek and humble Lamb of God." (Humility, Andrew Murray, pg 7,8.)[21]

Meekness means 'no retaliation.' Usually we relate meekness with our relationship with people, but in the Scripture meekness is related even more to our relationship with God. This is the reason we must never rise up in retaliation against God who is the allower of our situations. We must demonstrate meekness toward God…Jesus was meek towards His Father. He was a willing Lamb who surrendered up His life when His Father asked Him. 'It pleased the Lord to bruise him; he hath put him to grief' (Isaiah 53:10) The Lord Jesus knew it was the will of the Father to suffer shame and disgrace, and then be rejected and slain. Jesus always delighted to do His Father's will. He had no anger towards His Heavenly Father. Anger is the opposite of meekness. Anger is symptomatic of unsurrendered rights."[22]

There comes a time when you have to be prepared to lay down everything we are, and allow others to mock, humiliate, criticise and be abusive to us. When this happens, our reaction is usually to defend ourselves. It is at this time that we have to take cognisance of the example of Jesus Christ as He was led through His mock trials, before the Sanhedrin and also the Roman officials.

The interesting thing about all the accusations is whilst most of them were factual, they had been perverted to present the facts in a way that degraded the Son of God and added credibility to the Pharisees. All the facts had been taken out of context. Jesus had said that He would rebuild *this Temple* in three days. He was referring to His body, but the "judges and jury" refused to listen with their spiritual ears and hearts to the message of the Son of God. We must be aware of what we are listening to, test the words, and accept them when they are from God.

The servant's heart is completely surrendered to the will of the Father to understanding that He sees the end result of everything. We may have habits or friends that are taking the Lord's place in our lives. These need to be surrendered.

Isaiah 55:8-9,
> ⁸ "For My thoughts *are* not your thoughts,
> Nor *are* your ways My ways," says the Lord.
> ⁹ "For *as* the heavens are higher than the earth,
> So are My ways higher than your ways,
> And My thoughts than your thoughts. [23]

Perhaps the hardest lesson to learn with regards to humility and meekness comes during trials. The Epistle of James refers to these trials, and he encourages us to count them pure joy (James 1:2). James continues, in verse three of the same chapter, to advise us that these trials work patience in us. Unfortunately, some of these trials do not feel momentary, and it is really difficult to face the death of a loved one and see this as a short trial, caused to work a measure of patience in us.

It is during these trials that we have to learn to accept, as did Job, that God is greater than satan. God has everything under His command. Satan can do nothing that has not been approved by God for our instruction, admonition and correction. This, by the way, has nothing to do with temptation, as we see in James 1:13. God never tempts us with evil, but He does allow situations that try our faith and test the purity of our hearts (See Deuteronomy 8).

LONG-SUFFERING
Long-suffering has also been translated as patience in various translations of the Bible. Long-suffering, as well as being a fruit of the Spirit, is a quality required in the servant's heart. Long-suffering means exactly that - enduring or suffering a long time. This is a quality built into each one of us as we recognise that God is long-suffering with us. He does not give up on us and the hope that we will be conformed to the image of Christ.

Long-suffering is not taught to us during times of absolute bliss on earth (apparently, there are times like this!!), but it is learned as we experience trials that seem to go indefinitely, and we learn to endure the mental, physical and spiritual agony, and to appreciate what God endures with us.

The one with the servant's heart learns these attributes and is able to endure with people who are obstinate, arrogant, possessive, malicious and worse. This understanding comes as the servant hearted one realises the person's real needs seen through the eyes of God - through the filter of God's love. We must understand all people are able to come to the knowledge of Christ as Saviour, and so treat them as potential children of the King – His chosen ones. The fact they presently reject Him must not taint our perception of them.

This idea can be seen through the life of Saul who later became Paul. Can you imagine how you would feel if this man had chased your family and friends around the country, if he had killed and murdered many of them; was constantly maligning their beliefs; was intent on discrediting the life and teaching, and blasphemed against everything you were trying to teach your children, and if then, he had the audacity to say that he was doing this to protect your reputation.

This is exactly what Saul did. He ran riot trying to stamp out Christianity because, as a Jew, he believed that God the Father was the only One to be worshipped, and that the Messiah had not yet come. Saul did not believe that Jesus was the Messiah. He believed that God was being blasphemed by Jesus' claim of Sonship. Paul, therefore, persecuted the believers until God confronted him and changed his attitude.

God demonstrated longsuffering by forgiving Saul, and allowed him to become one of the most famous apostles of the New Testament. This is an example of the servant heart's requirement of long-suffering.

When we look at the life of Paul, it is interesting to note his complete conviction in what he believed. How many of us would consider signing a petition against the abuse of children or rape, but rather ignore the situation than actually stand up for what we believe in? What are we doing about the New Age movement and Pagan religions? The truth is, we are ignoring them and the plight of those in bondage.

Gideon should not be our example. He had an angel appear to him and call him a mighty man of God, a man of valour – he was hiding wheat in a wine-press. After killing a goat, and making a broth and unleavened bread, Gideon returned to find the angel still waiting for him to bring the sacrifice to offer up to God. The angel told Gideon to pour out the broth and place the meat and bread on a stone. Immediately, fire came from the stone, burned up the sacrifice and the angel then went up into Heaven (Judges 6:11-21). After this, Gideon tested God and put out his fleeces two nights in a row to see if it really was God talking! (Judges 6:36-40). Whilst it is right to test the words we receive, we must be aware that submitting to fear and anxiety will rob us of our faith in God. We know that without faith it is impossible to please God (Hebrews 11:6). God exhibited long-suffering towards Gideon by not becoming angry and frustrated. I, like Moses, would have been tempted to hit Gideon with a stick instead of speaking to the "rock" in front of me!

Moses had times where he exhibited long-suffering on behalf of his people. A hike of forty years had to be a measure of this. But we know that Moses was not allowed to enter the land of Canaan because of the episode where, in disobedience to God, he hit the rock instead of speaking to it. If anyone had needed the chariot of fire, it should have been Moses, at that moment. Moses had the pleasure of leading the Israelites out of Egypt, but then had to fight every step of the way to encourage the people to remain in the desert and stay faithful to God. The extent to which Moses made the exhibit long-suffering is seen in the many times that he pleaded with God on behalf of Israel. The extent to which Moses made the decision to exhibit long-suffering is seen in the many times he pleaded with God on behalf of Israel. Moses would rather have taken on Israel's punishment and died, than have Israel reap her just rewards from God. Twice, Moses asked God how His Name would be tarnished if the nation were wiped out because of their rebellion and backsliding. Moses was prepared to be their sacrifice in these times, in an effort to spare Israel from the wrath of God. (Numbers 14:11-19)

God exhibited the servants heart of long-suffering when He called to Ephraim:

Hosea 11:8-11

> [8] "How can I give you up, Ephraim?
> *How* can I hand you over, Israel?
> How can I make you like Admah?
> *How* can I set you like Zeboiim?
> My heart churns within Me;
> My sympathy is stirred.
>
> [9] I will not execute the fierceness of My anger;
> I will not again destroy Ephraim.
> For I *am* God, and not man,
> The Holy One in your midst;
> And I will not come with terror.
>
> [10] "They shall walk after the Lord.
> He will roar like a lion.
> When He roars,
> Then *His* sons shall come trembling from the west;
>
> [11] They shall come trembling like a bird from Egypt,
> Like a dove from the land of Assyria.
> And I will let them dwell in their houses,"
>   Says the Lord.[24]

God taught Ephraim to walk; He held the people in His arms. He had helped them grow up, and they had rejected Him; but the Father still loved them, and still called out to them.

Hosea 11:3-4

> [3] "I taught Ephraim to walk,
> Taking them by their arms;
> But they did not know that I healed them.
> [4] I drew them with gentle cords,
> With bands of love,
> And I was to them as those who take the yoke from their neck.

> I stooped *and* fed them.[25]

We would probably decided on 'tough love', or sent the wayward child to a chidren's home and allow the juvenile court structures to deal with the problem. God, on the other hand, does not need a Plan B for us when we rebel. He allows us to continue, although He places a hedge around us as He takes us into the wilderness so we may see and learn that it is better in the arms of our Father.

Hosea 2:6-8
> [6] "Therefore, behold,
> I will hedge up your way with thorns,
> And wall her in,
> So that she cannot find her paths.
> [7] She will chase her lovers,
> But not overtake them;
> Yes, she will seek them, but not find *them*.
> Then she will say,
> 'I will go and return to my first husband,
> For then *it was* better for me than now.'
> [8] For she did not know
> That I gave her grain, new wine, and oil,
> And multiplied her silver and gold—
> *Which* they prepared for Baal.[26]

God also exhibited long-suffering with possibly the most saddest man in the Bible - Elijah. This prophet of God defeated the prophets of Baal in a manner that I would love to see happen today (Refer 1 Kings 18). Just imagine walking up a hill, allowing the pagan prophets to scream, cut themselves and shout for half the day. Then imagine setting up a sacrifice, dousing it with barrels of water, and ask God to set it on fire.

The pagan prophets had thought that Elijah's God would be as powerless as theirs. Elijah went on to announce the end of the drought which had been plagued Israel for the last three years.

Having shown the Lord God as mighty, Elijah then proceeded to execute all 850 pagan prophets. then, with Jezebel angry, he escaped to hide in the wilderness. When Elijah stopped running, he told God to kill him (1 Kings 19:4). He should have stayed near Jezebel if he had wanted to die!
Elijah reminds us of how human we are, that after a mighty victory for God, there is usually a feeling of anti-climax. God uses us mightily, and a few seconds later sink into the doldrums of depression. God's long-suffering is something we should be grateful for.

The following verses in Colossians give a perfect yardstick for the servant's heart.

Colossians 3:12-17,

¹² Therefore, as *the* elect of God, holy and beloved, put on tender mercies, kindness, humility, meekness, longsuffering; ¹³ bearing with one another, and forgiving one another, if anyone has a complaint against another; even as Christ forgave you, so you also *must do*. ¹⁴ But above all these things put on love, which is the bond of perfection. ¹⁵ And let the peace of God rule in your hearts, to which also you were called in one body; and be thankful. ¹⁶ Let the word of Christ dwell in you richly in all wisdom, teaching and admonishing one another in psalms and hymns and spiritual songs, singing with grace in your hearts to the Lord. ¹⁷ And whatever you do in word or deed, *do* all in the name of the Lord Jesus, giving thanks to God the Father through Him.[27]

BROKENNESS AND CONTRITENESS

Psalm 51 is the perfect example of the servant's heart in action. Let us take an in-depth look into the Psalm and envisage the experiences David went through, and consider how we can associate this Psalm with our own change of heart. David wrote this Psalm after Nathan the prophet had come to him and confronted David with the sin of adultery with Bathsheba.

Psalm 51:1,
> Have mercy upon me, O God,
> According to Your lovingkindness;
> > According to the multitude of Your tender mercies,
> > Blot out my transgressions. [28]

In the first verse, David is calling on the mercy of the Lord. the word *chanan* (mercy) means to be favourable, kind, gracious; to pity, have mercy; to bestow; to complain; to make lovely; to implore; to seek mercy. This word was often used in the context of the strong negotiating with the weak.

David then referred to the tender mercies of the Lord, *Racham*, (tender mercies) has the meaning of compassion, mercy, sympathy, tenderness, pity and tender love. David knew that these were the characteristics of God's mercy, and he called on God to show His mercy.

The word used to refer to the blotting out of the transgressions, *Machah*, means to wipe; wipe off; to blot out; to be wiped off; be removed; and to put away. David understood that when his sins were wiped clean, there was no record of them remaining.

The word used for transgressions, *Pesha*, means a revolt (national, moral or religious); transgression, sin, a trespass; wickedness, rebellion, faithlessness, apostasy, defection, and the guilt of rebellious sin. David knew that his sin with Bathsheba had been one of rebellion, and he made no pretence of asking God to forgive a sin other than the sin of rebellion. David should have been away at war with his soldiers. As human beings, we usually are not quick to see the consequences of our behaviour, yet aferwars stand amazed at out blindness.

Psalm 51:2,
> ² Wash me thoroughly from my iniquity,
> And cleanse me from my sin.[29]

The word used for wash, *kāvas*, means to trample, tread; to wash, bleach, cleanse; to be washed; to be purified. the ancient method of laundering required treading with the feet, kneading, and beating the clothes in cold water. David was not expecting his cleansing and washing to be like the act of baptism today. David was expecting to be handled like we would handle a carpet that needed the dust beaten out of it – a gentle shake does not do the job. Unfortunately, we have taken the idea of washing our sins to be like that of a super washing powder; where all you do is dip the dirty clothes in the water, and gently lift them out; no washing, no rubbing, no scrubbing. We have allowed the idea of God's sanctifying scrubbing session to become a bubble bath.

The word for cleanse, *nāqāh*, means to absolve; declare innocent; acquit and pardon. It contains the idea of no longer having an obligation of responsibility. David acknowledged his sin, and was aware that, unless he had been cleansed and pardoned from it, that sin would continue to haunt him. Whilst David was forgiven, he still had to bear the consequences of his actions. The child from the adulterous union died, and various other family reperscussions followed.

Psalm 51:3-4
> ³ For I acknowledge my transgressions,
> And my sin *is* always before me.
> ⁴ Against You, You only, have I sinned,
> And done *this* evil in Your sight—
> That You may be found just when You speak,
> *And* blameless when You judge.[30]

David knew his sin was only ever against God, and because of this his repentance had to be directed towards God. He knew that God was just, lawful, and righteous, and when injustice prevailed, God was the only one who could and would be just. David was aware that God was, and remains, the righteous judge, our arbitrator; the one who has the right to administer vindication or condemnation.

Psalm 51:5-6
> ⁵ Behold, I was brought forth in iniquity,
> And in sin my mother conceived me.
> ⁶ Behold, You desire truth in the inward parts,
> And in the hidden *part* You will make me to know wisdom.[31]

David understood the concept of mankind being born in sin, but also that God finds pleasure, takes delight in, and is pleased with truth in our inner being. The wisdom that God will grant to us as we seek Him in our hidden parts includes knowledge, experience, intelligence, insight and judgement. Both wisdom and truth are attributes of God Himself.

Psalm 51:7-9
> [7] Purge me with hyssop, and I shall be clean;
> Wash me, and I shall be whiter than snow.
> [8] Make me hear joy and gladness,
> *That* the bones You have broken may rejoice.
> [9] Hide Your face from my sins,
> And blot out all my iniquities.[32]

David understood to be made clean by God would result in his being morally pure, clean and innocent of his sin. We are not able to purify ourselves; this is an act that only God can do for us. When David asked to be able to hear joy and gladness, the hearing was to be with an undivided attention or obedience. The broken bones that David referred to here can also be paralleled to a broken heart, as David was filled with remorse for the broken fellowship with God which he experienced. The word for bones can also be translated as essence, or self – here, the very make-up of David himself, not necessarily just his physical body.

Sin is a turning away from God, whilst the word *iniquity* includes the consequences of the sins committed. The purging with hyssop was symbolic of the cleansing use of hyssop. This was the herb used to clean the Temple, and also to smear the door posts with the blood of the lamb at the first Passover when the Israelites left Egypt.

Psalm 51:10
> [10] Create in me a clean heart, O God,
> And renew a steadfast spirit within me.[33]

The word used for create, *bārā*, means to create, form, make, produce; to cut; to engrave; to carve. This word also possesses the meaning of "bringing into existence", implying that this object did not exist before the experience David asked for in his own life. This *bārā*, is the same word used in Genesis Chapter one: "In the beginning, God created..." This means that the new heart David received was one which was an entirely new creation; he did not have the old one pressed into the correct shape; he had received a brand new heart; one that would continually follow the Law of the Lord.

Ezekiel 36:26-27
[26] I will give you a new heart and put a new spirit within you; I will take the heart of stone out of your flesh and give you a heart of flesh. [27] I will put My Spirit within you and cause you to walk in My statutes, and you will keep My judgments and do *them*.[34]

The word used for heart her, *lev,* means the blood-pumping organ of the body, although it is more commonly used for the totality of mans inner or immaterial nature. These are the deepest innermost human feelings.

The renewing of a right spirit involves the Breath of God as He breathes into the nostrils of the man He has created again. (Refer the section on *bārā*, which explains re the creation.) This is the same as when God breathed into Adam's nostrils in the Garden of Eden.

Psalm 51:11
> [11] Do not cast me away from Your presence,
> And do not take Your Holy Spirit from me.[35]

The restoration process concerning the joy of salvation is God's method to draw us Israel back to Himself. This would include all the Laws of Restorsation in the Old Testament. God always restores more than the original amount. (Exodus 22:4)

The word *shuv*, (restore), means to cause to return, lead back, seduce, revoke, and is best illustrated with the returning of the sundial in 2 Kings 20:10. That miracle was never undone; God restored that time for Hezekiah - it was revoked.

Psalm 51:12-14
> [12] Restore to me the joy of Your salvation,
> And uphold me *by Your* generous Spirit.
>
> [13] *Then* I will teach transgressors Your ways,
> And sinners shall be converted to You.
>
> [14] Deliver me from the guilt of bloodshed, O God,
> The God of my salvation,
> *And* my tongue shall sing aloud of Your righteousness.[36]

David promised to lead others to the courts of God and tell of God's good deeds. This is not a manipulation on David's behalf; this was thankfulness and gratefulness from deep within his heart because he knew that he was forgiven.

Psalm 51:15
> [15] O Lord, open my lips,
> And my mouth shall show forth Your praise.[37]

David desired the Lord to open his lips and fill his mouth with praise to God. David understood that the mouth can be used for perversity and for good, and he encouraged the Lord to fill his mouth with praise to God.

Psalm 51:16-17
> [16] For You do not desire sacrifice, or else I would give *it;*
> You do not delight in burnt offering.
> [17] The sacrifices of God *are* a broken spirit,
> A broken and a contrite heart—
> These, O God, You will not despise.[38]

In a prophetic utterance, David acknowledged that whilst God was still receiving the sacrifices offered at the altars by the Levites, this was not what God desired. David knew that to God, the person's heart attitude was far more important than any number of sacrificial bulls, goats or sheep.

The word *shavar*, means to be broken, smashed, demolished, torn into pieces, broken by penitence. It was also used to denote a shattered heart. David knew God was not interested in a fake heart change – the human heart, its emotions, desires, plans and decisions, must be completely destroyed so that God can begin His cretion of a new heart.

Psalm 51:18-19
> [18] Do good in Your good pleasure to Zion;
> Build the walls of Jerusalem.
> [19] Then You shall be pleased with the sacrifices of righteousness,
> With burnt offering and whole burnt offering;
> Then they shall offer bulls on Your altar. [39]

David is here referring to the infinite goodness of God, and the rebuilding of Jerusalem. We know that this passage has prophetic significance with regards to the New Jerusalem, when Christ shall return. David understood that when the people offered righteous sacrifices to God, they would again be pleasing to God.

PEACE
Isaiah 32:16-20,
> [16] Then justice will dwell in the wilderness,
> And righteousness remain in the fruitful field.
>
> [17] The work of righteousness will be peace,
> And the effect of righteousness, quietness and assurance forever.
>
> [18] My people will dwell in a peaceful habitation,
> In secure dwellings, and in quiet resting places,
>
> [19] Though hail comes down on the forest,
> And the city is brought low in humiliation.
>
> [20] Blessed *are* you who sow beside all waters,
> Who send out freely the feet of the ox and the donkey. [40]

John 14:27

[27] Peace I leave with you, My peace I give to you; not as the world gives do I give to you. Let not your heart be troubled, neither let it be afraid. [41]

Peace is probably the most controversial issue in the world. Discussions over peace cause wars. Peace can never be acquainted with a fatalistic attitude. Peace is not a suicidal submission to the circumstance of life.

Peace is the deep inner knowledge that all is well. It is the conviction within you which says that no matter what is happening around you, God is still in control of all situations. Peace comes from a relationship with Jesus Christ - that assurance that nothing can separate you from the love of God, as Paul quoted:

Romans 8:38-39
[38] For I am persuaded that neither death nor life, nor angels nor principalities nor powers, nor things present nor things to come, [39] nor height nor depth, nor any other created thing, shall be able to separate us from the love of God which is in Christ Jesus our Lord.[42]

When this verse becomes a revelation, there will be nothing that can turn your world upside down and make you lose your peace. The servant's heart requires this kind of peace; especially as we experience the process of separation and the time of change in our hearts. We cannot experience the fullness of change in our own lives unless we are prepared to submit to every part of the pruning that Jesus will require during the heart transplant period. Unless you experience the fellowship of Jesus Christ and His peace, you will not survive the process. You have to be prepared that this process could involve the stripping away of everything that you hold dear in life. To loose and submit in giving up everything, will require a definite peace as you hand over your life unconditionally to Jesus.

AUTHORITY
"As faith is the principle by which we obtain life, so obedience is the principle by which that life is lived out... In order to recover authority, obedience must first be restored... Since all authorities come from God we must learn to obey them all... Sooner or later, those who serve God must meet authority in the universe, in society, in the home, in the Church. How can one serve and obey God if he has never met the authority of God?

> *Let us therefore learn a few lessons:*
> 1. *Have a spirit of obedience.*
> 2. *Practise obedience.*
> 3. *Learn to exercise delegated authority -once you have learned how to be under God's authority, you will count yourself as nothing even after God entrusts you with much.*
>
> *Some only learn obedience, and fail to know how to be in authority when they are sent to some place to work. It is necessary to learn how both to be under authority and in authority. The Church suffers from many who do not know how to obey, but she is likewise damaged through some who have not learned how to be in authority."*[43]

Thus far in the study on the servant's heart, we have discussed various attributes that need to be relinquished, as well as those attributes that need to be cultivated. Obedience to God's Word and Will are of the utmost importance. These should be embraced above any personal sacrifice which may be required.

When we read the account in Leviticus 10:1-7 of Aaron's sons offering the strange fire, we see that, whilst these were two of the original four sons of Aaron anointed for the priesthood by Moses, they decided to offer their own offering of fire and incense to the Lord. This disobedient behaviour resulted in their death.

Looking at the strange fire offered by the sons of Aaron as constituting a different incense than the one commissioned by the Lord, we see a type of man's attempt to make use of his own flesh to accomplish God's works. Included in that would be actions such as counselling in situations outside our calling or anointing and prophesying out of our own wisdom, and could even extent to praying for circumstances which we do not fully understand, almost trying to manipulate God because we only have half of the picture. Strange fire can be likened to preaching from habit, or delivering sermons which are not what the Lord is leading the congregation.

When we recognise the calling of ministry on our lives, it is not for us to go out and set that calling. When a vision is given, the timing must coincide with God's timing. We will suffer loss if we try to implement our own calling.

True authority comes from God alone, and He will allow each of us to find favour with men and circumstances in His time. When we receive these promises, they are to be written on our hearts, but they are not for us to promote.

As with Elisha, we need to learn to be in submission and serve for a long time. Obedience to God, His statutes, laws and precepts, precedes change in our authority status.

The most perfect example of being subjected to authority, and being in authority was Jesus Christ Himself, He knew He had the authority over demons, but He also knew His responsibility to obey His Father's will.

1 Peter 2:13-17

[13] Therefore submit yourselves to every ordinance of man for the Lord's sake, whether to the king as supreme, [14] or to governors, as to those who are sent by him for the punishment of evildoers and *for the* praise of those who do good. [15] For this is the will of God, that by doing good you may put to silence the ignorance of foolish men— [16] as free, yet not using liberty as a cloak for vice, but as bondservants of God. [17] Honor all *people*. Love the brotherhood. Fear God. Honor the king.[44]

CHAPTER 2
WHAT CHARACTERISTICS SHOULD THE SERVANT'S HEART BE WITHOUT?

PRIDE
The Oxford dictionary describes pride as being of a high opinion of ones own qualities and merits, having a sense of what benefits ones position.

Pride is to consider an act for a fellow believer below ones station.

Proverbs 1:5,
⁵ A wise *man* will hear and increase learning, And a man of understanding will attain wise counsel,[45]

Proverbs 11:2,
² When pride comes, then comes shame;
But with the humble *is* wisdom.[46]

Proverbs 11:20-21,
²⁰ Those who are of a perverse heart *are* an abomination to the Lord,
But *the* blameless in their ways *are* His delight.
²¹ *Though they join* forces, the wicked will not go unpunished;
But the posterity of the righteous will be delivered.[47]

Pride can have no place in the servant's heart, because as the servant learns to yield daily to the unctioning of the Holy Spirit, he realises that pride limits the working of the Holy Spirit. If our pride will not allow us to as**sociate** with certain people, we will limit ministry for the Lord.

LEGALISM
The Oxford Dictionary defines legalism as being an exaltation of the law or red tape, a preference of the Law over the Gospel; the doctrine of justification by works.

We often find ourselves doing things because we are bound by legalism. We consider what is legally right, and hold rigidly to that. We submit to these laws because we want to impress God. God is not impressed when we hide behind the laws like the Pharisees did.

Many people think by tithing, keeping the traffic and tax laws, going to Church, attending Sunday School etc. etc. they are conforming to the desires of God. This is not true. If we only behave in this manner because we have been taught it is the correct way to behave, we are following a system of legalism. Christian life and behaviour must ultimately be a result of revelation from God and His Word.

Legalism undermines love. If we obey God's Word through legalism, (meaning we do what we are told because we are trying to be obedient), then we are not obeying God because we are obeying God's Word out of love. We shoud naturally obey God's Word out of the depth of our love for Him. It is not a thought process; it is a heart action. If going to Church on Sunday becomes a ritual that loses the excitement and expectancy to meet God and fellowship with God's people; it is mere legalism. Legalism detracts from the personal relationship which God desires with each one of us.

Hosea 6:6,
⁶ For I desire mercy and not sacrifice,
And the knowledge of God more than burnt offerings.[48]

Legalism dictates that as long as we offer the correct sacrifices for sin, atonement offerings, fellowship and many others, we will satisfy God's Will. However, God desires that we check our hearts attitudes and make sure they are in line with God's desires and attitudes. Legalism is not God's desire - He examines the heart. An evil heart attitude was what was wrong with Cain's offering right in the beginning.

BITTERNESS
Bitterness is described in The Oxford Dictionary as being caused by or showing mental pain; full of affliction or resentment; virulent, relentless; biting and harsh.

Bitterness is caused by retaining the anger, hurt and humiliation of a previous experience and allowing it to taint current events and situations. Bitterness wards out the fear against the threat of being used or abused again, and attempts to hide from the vulnerability caused by the pain of the previous occasion.

The person with a servant's heart will be aware of past experiences, and will allow the Holy Spirit to heal and restore these areas in his life. This permits a process of continuous restoration, as in faith he has learns to trust the Holy Spirit. Forgiveness is the antidote for bitterness.

Smiths Bible Dictionary has this definition of gall:
Gall.
1.   *Mereerah*, denoting "that which is bitter"; hence the term is applied to the "bile" or "gall" (the fluid secreted by the liver), from its intense bitterness, Job

16:13; 20:25; it is also used of the "poison" of serpents, Job 20:14, which the ancients erroneously believed was their gall. 2. *Rôsh*, generally translated "gall" in the English Bible, is in Hos. 10:4 rendered "hemlock"; in Deut. 32:33 and Job 20:16, rôsh denotes the "poison" or "venom" of serpents. From Deut. 29:18 and Lam. 3:19, compared with Hos. 10:4, it is evident that the Hebrew term denotes some bitter and perhaps poisonous plant. Other writers have supposed, and with some reason, from Deut. 32:32, that some berry-bearing plant must be intended. Gesenius understands poppies; in which case the gall mingled with the wine offered to our Lord at his crucifixion, and refused by him, would be an anæsthetic, and tend to diminish the sense of suffering. Dr. Richardson, "Ten Lectures on Alcohol," p. 23, thinks these drinks were given to the crucified to diminish the suffering through their intoxicating effects.[49]

Michal, daughter of King Saul, demonstrated a prime example of bitterness. She was enraged by David's display of enthusiasm towards God, and allowed her resentment to become bitterness (2 Samuel 6:20-23). *Michal* married to David, had been taken from him by her father, given to someone else to marry. Later, she was returned to David (1 Samuel 25:44). These experiences clouded her appreciation of David, and consequently became barren for the rest of her life. Barrenness was the punishment for her bitterness. (1 Samuel 18:17-30; 1 Chronicles 15:29; 2 Samuel 6:20-23).

Hebrews 12:15

[15] looking carefully lest anyone fall short of the grace of God; lest any root of bitterness springing up cause trouble, and by this many become defiled;[50]

In the above verse, we see the effectys of bitterness. Because of bitterness, we may cause ourselves and others to fall short of the grace of God. Jesus said it would be better for us to tie a millstone around our necks and drown, than to cause any of the children of God to stumble (Matthew 18:6).

Bitterness is to be put off. This does not mean that you need deliverance ministry, inner healing, or pastoral counselling sessions for months on end; it is a decision you take to change the way you are. When Scripture tells us to 'put off', we are expected to change our behavioural patterns. Sure, this may entail some help and encouragement, and possibly even counselling, to understand and talk through some circumstances that have occurred in but this does not give us a licence to carry hurt and anger around in your hearts.

Acts 8:23,
[23] For I see that you are poisoned by bitterness and bound by iniquity."[51]

Ephesians 4:31

[31] Let all bitterness, wrath, anger, clamor, and evil speaking be put away from you, with all malice.[52]

Hebrews 12:14-15

[14] Pursue peace with all *people,* and holiness, without which no one will see the Lord: [15] looking carefully lest anyone fall short of the grace of God; lest any root of bitterness springing up cause trouble, and by this many become defiled;[53]

God expects you to start the process by renewing your mind. You decide to no longer harbour bitterness, and every time you become aware of it, you take it to the Lord in prayer and ask forgiveness. This is not a once-off decision but a personal lifestyle.

Some people choose to continue holding on to their bitterness; but, as we see in the life of Naomi, circumstances can and do change, and we should not hold onto the old hurts, but allow the new delights in the Lord to replace those scars. (See Book of Ruth)

Naomi had lost two children and a husband during the years she was exiled in a strange country due to severe famine in Israel. She had also inherited two daughters-in-law. When weighing up the pros and cons, Naomi decided she would be better off back in Israel. At first she was dutifully followed by both her daughters-in-law, but she pleaded with them, and one returned to her own parents. Naomi returned home to the town of Bethlehem, and promptly renamed herself *Marah*, meaning bitter. Naomi still believed in God, as shown by the fact that Ruth was converted and knew the Name of the Lord, but she focussed on her circumstances and not on God.

Despite Naomi's insistence on looking at circumstances, and not at the Lord of the circumstances, her life began to change. Within months she faced a completely new set of circumstances which eventually led her to become the Great-grandmother of King David.

We often do not see the reasons for the circumstances we face and well-meaning individuals might tell us they are designed to give us stronger characters. But we always must remember God is in control. To dwell on how bad things are, and that they probably cannot get any worse, is only allowing ourselves to wallow in self pity, which can lead us into areas of resentment and bitterness.

We read how Naomi encouraged her daughter-in-law to follow the customs of the Israelites and approach her kinsmen-redeemer. Naomi realised that unless she started to change her attitude and position, she would remain in the depths of despair. She, like David her great-grandson, knew to set her heart on the Lord and not allow herself to remain downcast. (Psalm 43:5)

When Naomi's heart attitude was changed, she opened the door for many circumstantial changes. Had she remained resentful and bitter, she may never have sent Ruth to Boaz's field, nor encouraged Ruth to ask for Boaz's protection.

Naomi could very well have become a hindrance to Ruth's future by harbouring bitterness, but she became resourceful, and secured protection both for herself and for Ruth. If we insist on entertaining bitterness we shall reap the bitter rewards.

On occasion, David became downcast; but he shows us how he picked himself up by praising the Lord.

Psalm 43:5,
> [5] Why are you cast down, O my soul?
> And why are you disquieted within me?
> Hope in God;
> For I shall yet praise Him,
> The help of my countenance and my God.[54]

1 Samuel 30:6,

[6] Now David was greatly distressed, for the people spoke of stoning him, because the soul of all the people was grieved, every man for his sons and his daughters. But David strengthened himself in the Lord his God.[55]

Peter Marshall wrote this prayer against bitterness:

Lord Jesus, Thou knowest me altogether. Thou knowest that I have steadily refused to forgive this one who has wronged me, yet have had the audacity often to seek Thy forgiveness for my own wrongdoing.

The acids of bitterness and a vengeful spirit have threatened to eat away my peace. Yet I have stubbornly rationalized every unlovely motive. I have said, "I am clearly in the right. It is only human to dislike a few people. This one deserves no forgiveness." How well I know that neither have I ever deserved the forgiveness which Thou hast always freely granted me.

So, Lord Jesus, I ask Thee now for the grace to forgive this hurt....
And, Lord, I give to Thee this emotion of resentment which clings as if glued to my heart. Wrest it from me. Cleanse every petty thought.
For these great mercies I thank Thee, in Thy name, who gave me the supreme example in forgiving even those who slew Thee.
Amen.[56]

ANGER
The Oxford Dictionary describes anger as an extreme displeasure.

Anger is, of course, a strong spirit of dislike or animosity, a vengeful spirit, a settled feeling of hatred.
Wrath describes an intense form of anger, probably involving violent outbursts.
Malice is wicked conduct toward another with the idea of harming his person

or reputation. It is an unreasonable dislike that takes pleasure in seeing others suffer.[57]

Proverbs 16:32,
> [32] *He who is* slow to anger *is* better than the mighty,
> And he who rules his spirit than he who takes a city.[58]

Proverbs 22:24-25,
> [24] Make no friendship with an angry man,
> And with a furious man do not go,
> [25] Lest you learn his ways
> And set a snare for your soul.[59]

When we allow ourselves to become angry at the actions of others because they do not correspond with the image we have set in our minds as our rights, we are definitely not showing the servant's heart.

Our hearts must become so malleable and soft, that we do not consider our own likes and dislikes, but rather are willing to endure whatever it takes to lead another soul to Christ, to serve our Master with all our being.

Anger is usually expressed in some way, and this has the ability to lead us into sin. Anger, when released because of the hardness of our hearts, can cause us to sin against the Father.

Jesus at the sales tables in the Temple, beautifully expressed anger on behalf of those suffering injustice because of a direct disregard for the laws and ordinances of God. His expression of anger was without sin. Jesus responded to the disregard and corruption of His Father's House with righteous indignation. In no way whatsoever did Jesus sin; something which we may not achieve instantly! (Mark 11:15–17; Luke 19:45-46; Matthew 21:12-14; John 2:13-17)

How do we put Jesus' action into context today? Firstly, if you arrive home and bump the car, fall over the cat and close your finger in the front door, you are not justified in turning over the dining room table in anger. However, if you arrive home one evening and find your daughter reading tarot cards on the dining room table, you have every right to take drastic action! The difference is that God is involved. Your reaction is due to the assault against God's sovereignty by the evil associated with the tarot cards in your home, and not because you had a bad day.

How you handle the situation is another challenge you will have to account for.

Jonah had other issues. He had been called to Ninevah to speak the Word of the Lord and he had run away. After returning and finally giving God's Word finally to the people, they repented, and God did not destroy them. Jonah was then angry with God. Following this, when the plant for shade sprung up next to where Jonah was moping in self-pity, he was really grateful. However, after that, he became angry again when the plant died the next day. In this way, God showed Jonah how his anger was inappropriate.

Jonah 3:10-4:1

[10] Then God saw their works, that they turned from their evil way; and God relented from the disaster that He had said He would bring upon them, and He did not do it. But it displeased Jonah exceedingly, and he became angry.[60]

Jonah 4:9-11

[9] Then God said to Jonah, "*Is it* right for you to be angry about the plant?" And he said, "*It is* right for me to be angry, even to death!" [10] But the Lord said, "You have had pity on the plant for which you have not labored, nor made it grow, which [a]came up in a night and perished in a night. [11] And should I not pity Nineveh, that great city, in which are more than one hundred and twenty thousand persons who cannot discern between their right hand and their left—and much livestock?"[61]

LIST OF PAST HURTS / SELF-PITY
Christians share comfort. God's comfort is not *given*; it is *loaned*, and you are expected to pass it on to others. The pain you experience now will help you encourage others in their trials. When you suffer, avoid self-pity, for self-pity will make you a reservoir instead of a channel. If you fail to share God's comfort with others, your experience in the furnace will be wasted; and it is a tragic thing to waste your sufferings.[62]

Comparing each new experience with past hurts, as a way of avoiding new hurts, becomes a major stumbling block in our lives. Whether we have been hurt crossing a road, and need the visual and emotional assistance of a Zebra crossing or traffic light, or we have been abused by one whom we thought was a good friend, we all judge new situations based on our memroeis of past ones. We need to allow the Holy Spirit to renew our minds by the 'washing of the water of the Word' (Ephesians 5:26) so we can be the new creatures in Christ we were destined to be (2 Corinthians 5:17) and not the result of human failures.

Retaining a memory 'hit list' hinders the healing and restorative process which the Holy Spirit would do in our lives, and through us to heal others.

Unhealed wounds become suppurating sores that are toxic to our entire spiritual being, poisoning our appreciation for everything God has done and promises to do. This can also lead to self-indulgent pity and introspection.

Some proudly display their emotional scars as though they were going to receive recognition for them. This reminds me of the praying Pharisee who, Jesus said, had already received his reward. We must be sure that our testimonies give the glory to God, and not our survival ability.

The eighth chapter of Romans gives us some insight into the workings of pain.

DIVINE COUNSEL FOR OUR PAIN		
REFERENCE	THE WORKINGS OF PAIN	GOD'S COUNSEL TO US
Romans 8:1 Romans 8:18 Romans 8:26 Romans 8:31 Romans 8:37	Pain comes from accusation. Pain causes us to be short-sighted. Pain obscures the possibility of hope. Pain tends to convince us that we are by ourselves. Pain causes us to be stopped by undesirable circumstances.	Live according to the Spirit. Look for the glory that will be revealed. The Holy Spirit ministers to us and through us in prayer. Realize the presence of God in our lives. Realize that we are more thank conquerors through Jesus Christ [63]

Isaiah 43:18-19
> [18] "Do not remember the former things,
> Nor consider the things of old.
> [19] Behold, I will do a new thing,
> Now it shall spring forth;
> Shall you not know it?
> I will even make a road in the wilderness
> And rivers in the desert.[64]

God's promise here is to make a way in areas we have no ideas of how to fix. That is one of God's specialities. We have to learn to trust Him and allow Him to make new paths for us.

The person with a servant's heart would, in this instance, count his own experiences as least important, and focus on what the Lord has done, and how to best serve the Lord during his brief period on earth.

Paul had the most amazing list of accomplishments as far as disappointments were concerned. He listed some of them as such:

2 Corinthians 4:8-9

⁸ *We are* hard-pressed on every side, yet not crushed; *we are* perplexed, but not in despair; ⁹ persecuted, but not forsaken; struck down, but not destroyed—[65]

Paul could have given up on more than one occasion. He was beaten by his own Roman guards, rejected by the Jews and disciples, and the list continues, but he never gave up.

SELF-RIGHTEOUSNESS

If, as model citizens of this world, we rely our own good behaviour, we become self-righteous. Tithing, giving to the poor, paying taxes and even attending Church can cause us to feel we are better than others. This form of legalism hardens our hearts to God's Spirit as we consider ourselves 'righteous' before God. This is not essential Christianity.

Isaiah 64:6,

⁶ But we are all like an unclean *thing,*
And all our righteousnesses *are* like filthy rags;
We all fade as a leaf,
And our iniquities, like the wind,
Have taken us away.[66]

Proverbs 30:12

¹² *There is* a generation *that is* pure in its own eyes,
Yet is not washed from its filthiness.[67]

Galatians 3:16,

¹⁶ Now to Abraham and his Seed were the promises made. He does not say, "And to seeds," as of many, but as of one, "And to your Seed," who is Christ.[68]

1 John 3:10,

¹⁰ In this the children of God and the children of the devil are manifest: Whoever does not practice righteousness is not of God, nor *is* he who does not love his brother.[69]

There is no place for self-righteousness in the servant's heart. We stand before the throne of God by grace; clothed in the robes of righteousness given to us by Jesus Christ.

SELF-JUSTIFICATION

Self-justification is the idea that if we have sufficient reasons opr excuses, we are entitled to misbehave, and God must have sympathy for us.. Rubbish! We cannot justify our behaviour now by our past. Satan and sin rule this world, but that does not mean we should submit to his branding. We are in the world but not of the world.

Self-justification causes us to absolve ourselves of the consequences of our sins. The Holy Spirit will not work with those who determine to hold on to strongholds and sinful desires, however pious they may appear.

Proverbs 21:2,
> ² Every way of a man *is* right in his own eyes,
> But the Lord weighs the hearts.[70]

Three tests
"'Pride,' says Oswald Sanders, "is a sin of whose presence its victim is least conscious. There are however, three tests by means of which it can soon be discovered:
- *The test of precedence.* How do we react when another is selected for the assignment we expected, or for the office we coveted? When another is promoted and we are overlooked? When another outshines us in gifts and accomplishments.
- *The test of sincerity.* In our moments of honest self-criticism we will say many things about ourselves, and really mean them. But how do we feel when others, especially our rivals, say exactly the same things about us?
- *The test of criticism.* Does criticism arouse hostility and resentment in our hearts, and cause us to fly into immediate self-justification? [71]

FAVOURITISM / PARTIALITY
The servant's heart cannot allow itself the luxury of favouritism. This happens when we accept those people who are physically, financially or spiritually acceptable to us, but ostracise others because they do not fit the standard aqccepted in our circle.

Jesus Christ went out of His way to attract the those who would normally have been ostracised and rejected. Not many people willingly want to associate with to the town prostitute, but Jesus sought out those whom society rejected, and He gave them the opportunity of salvation.

Nobody would have stood a chance if God only chose the righteous. God loves every one of us unconditionally. He sent His Son to die for every single person. When we allow favouritism to have any part in our lives, we are considering ourselves above the wisdom and love of God. Because God forgives and forgets the sins of all those who come to Him in repentance, we do not have the rightr to consider ourselves better than the others.

Exodus 23:3,

³ You shall not show partiality to a poor man in his dispute.[72]

Deuteronomy 1:17,

¹⁷ You shall not show partiality in judgment; you shall hear the small as well as the great; you shall not be afraid in any man's presence, for the judgment *is*

God's. The case that is too hard for you, bring to me, and I will hear it.'[73]

Job 13:10,
> [10] He will surely rebuke you
> If you secretly show partiality.[74]

James 2:8-9,

[8] If you really fulfill *the* royal law according to the Scripture, "You shall love your neighbor as yourself," you do well; [9] but if you show partiality, you commit sin, and are convicted by the law as transgressors.[75]

SIN
We know from God's words to Cain, '... sin lies at the door" (Genesis 4:7), that sin's desire is for us, but we are also told that we should rule over it. Knowing full well that Jesus Christ died specifically for our sins ans His desire is that we sin no more, how do we explain the sin left in our lives.

Hebrews 10:11-14,

[11] And every priest stands ministering daily and offering repeatedly the same sacrifices, which can never take away sins. [12] But this Man, after He had offered one sacrifice for sins forever, sat down at the right hand of God, [13] from that time waiting till His enemies are made His footstool. [14] For by one offering He has perfected forever those who are being sanctified.[76]

Make sure you reread verse 14:

[14] For by one offering He has perfected forever those who are being sanctified.[77]

We are ALREADY perfected! Everyone is who accepts Christ as his Saviour! There are no more requirements for our sin to be taken away; we don't have to be washed again. We don't have to live in fear of sinning; we cannot do anything that would require more from Jesus. It is not possible.

But whilst we know we are more than conquerors (Romans 8:36-37), through distress, persecution, famine, nakedness, peril and the sword, there are also certain things that we have to put off - old habits and lifestyles.

Galatians 5:19-21,

[19] Now the works of the flesh are evident, which are: adultery, fornication, uncleanness, lewdness, [20] idolatry, sorcery, hatred, contentions, jealousies, outbursts of wrath, selfish ambitions, dissensions, heresies, [21] envy, murders, drunkenness, revelries, and the like; of which I tell you beforehand, just as I also told *you* in time past, that those who practice such things will not inherit the kingdom of God.[78]

Whilst there is no condemnation for those in Christ Jesus, as is so often quoted, we have to relaise that the complete verse reads the following way:

Romans 8:1,

There is therefore now no condemnation to those who are in Christ Jesus, who do not walk according to the flesh, but according to the Spirit.[79]

There is actually a small clause in the fine print concerning the fact we are not to be found walking in the flesh.

Many Christians are struggling with the servant's heart today because they have not put off the sin that so easily ensnares us and put on the new life in Christ.

Hebrews 12:1-6
Therefore we also, since we are surrounded by so great a cloud of witnesses, let us lay aside every weight, and the sin which so easily ensnares *us,* and let us run with endurance the race that is set before us, [2] looking unto Jesus, the author and finisher of *our* faith, who for the joy that was set before Him endured the cross, despising the shame, and has sat down at the right hand of the throne of God. [3] For consider Him who endured such hostility from sinners against Himself, lest you become weary and discouraged in your souls. [4] You have not yet resisted to bloodshed, striving against sin. [5] And you have forgotten the exhortation which speaks to you as to sons: "My son, do not despise the chastening of the Lord,
 nor be discouraged when you are rebuked by Him;

[6] For whom the Lord loves He chastens,
 and scourges every son whom He receives."[80]

And again

Ephesians 4:22-24

[22] that you put off, concerning your former conduct, the old man which grows corrupt according to the deceitful lusts, [23] and be renewed in the spirit of your mind, [24] and that you put on the new man which was created according to God, in true righteousness and holiness.[81]

The Book of Hebrews is quite clear about the consequences of a continued disregard of sin in the unrepentant Christian's life.

Hebrews 10:26-27,
[26] For if we sin willfully after we have received the knowledge of the truth, there no longer remains a sacrifice for sins, [27] but a certain fearful expectation of judgment, and fiery indignation which will devour the adversaries.[82]

And again:

Hebrews 10:29,

> ²⁹ Of how much worse punishment, do you suppose, will he be thought worthy who has trampled the Son of God underfoot, counted the blood of the covenant by which he was sanctified a common thing, and insulted the Spirit of grace?[83]

Here, Paul is explaining that if we deliberately continue in sin with no thought of repentance, we are in the act of pouring out Christ's Blood that was shed for the atonement of our sins, and are treading this precious commodity into the floor of the pigsty. We should not allow ourselves to continue in known sin, without repentance. True we are being made holy (Hebrews 2:11), and this is a continual process we undergo as a lifelong journey, but to be aware that we recognise something as sin does not give us licence to continue treading the precious Blood of Jesus underfoot just because we know the sin has already been paid for in full (Romans 6:1-2).

Hebrews 2:11,

¹¹ For both He who sanctifies and those who are being sanctified *are* all of one, for which reason He is not ashamed to call them brethren,[84]

Romans 6:1-2,

What shall we say then? Shall we continue in sin that grace may abound? ² Certainly not! How shall we who died to sin live any longer in it?[85]

Romans 6:15,

¹⁵ What then? Shall we sin because we are not under law but under grace? Certainly not![86]

This can so easily lead to condemnation, as we realise that we have fallen in an area on repeated occasion, but we have to accept that if we confess our sins, He is faithful and just to forgive us (1 John 1:9). The heart attitude is what counts here. Whilst we long to do the will of the Father, we find we have a war raging within us, and the things that we do not wish to do are the things that we find ourselves doing (Romans 7:15-16).

Then again, we find certain individuals who decide they may 'sin now and pray later'. Whilst we know we can come boldly to the throne room of grace, we have to be aware of the audacity inherent in the idea we can willingly sin and approach a Holy God and ask for forgiveness. Even with this kind of attitude, we must realise again, repentance means a turning away from the sin that holds us; we cannot expect to receive forgiveness if we insist on continuing on the path of sin that we have chosen. The receiving of forgiveness in this instance will require a change in heart, a complete return to God.

The problem is, the Church tends to use emotional blackmail with regards to sin, and will not accept the sinner into the fold unless he is washed, delivered, baptised, speaking in tongues, prophesying and displaying all the fruit of the Spirit.

Even Paul admitted to the war raging in his heart at the things he did not wish to do, and yet even Paul had to ask forgiveness when he fell. What about us? Are we allowing this holier-than-thou attitude to prevent us from accepting new converts into our midst? Are we allowing the Church to be painted as so wonderfully sanctified, that people who could be saved are scared off by our messages which do not encourage individuals in the fight against sin? Or, is the opposite true - that Christians are so scared of failing the requirements of the Church that sins are buried and not dealt with? How many people will openly admit to having problems with sin in their life when they are certain to be sent for exorcism instead of receiving the support and counsel which could change their lives and encourage a deeper relationship with Jesus?

How seriously bad is the subject of smoking for example? Sure it damages the temple, but what about the idea that if you do not encourage that believer, and you ostracise him because he smells of smoke, you are then a hypocrite because the person needs to experience God's love and acceptance, not the Churches legalistic doctrines, rules and regulations.

What if we were looking at a second-hand-car dealer? Just because most of them are swindlers (a classic example of what we are talking about – guilty by association!), does not mean we expect such a person to change profession before accepting him in the Body. We would encourage the person to start selling honestly, and to gain an honest reputation. Why then do we not extend this hand of reconciliation with regards to the sin in peoples lives?

We read in **Zechariah 3:1-5**, of the following vision,
Then he showed me Joshua the high priest standing before the Angel of the Lord, and Satan standing at his right hand to oppose him. **²** And the Lord said to Satan, "The Lord rebuke you, Satan! The Lord who has chosen Jerusalem rebuke you! *Is* this not a brand plucked from the fire?" **³** Now Joshua was clothed with filthy garments, and was standing before the Angel. **⁴** Then He answered and spoke to those who stood before Him, saying, "Take away the filthy garments from him." And to him He said, "See, I have removed your iniquity from you, and I will clothe you with rich robes." **⁵** And I said, "Let them put a clean turban on his head." So they put a clean turban on his head, and they put the clothes on him. And the Angel of the Lord stood by.[87]

When we read the above vision, we see a picture of how we stand before Jesus, and how He gives us new clothes and throws the filthy ones away. We also see the turban was changed - and this symbolises the changing and renewing of the mind. The only problem is, when you bath children, they immediately go and play in the mud, until such time as they learn that that activity is not desirable! As parents, we do not have robots that calmly sit down and never dirty their clothes; children need to grow and exercise their rights, and learn what is acceptable and what is not. You cannot expect a toddler to keep clean all day long. We, too, are also just like this; we have to return to the Saviour regularly and confess our sins, receive clean robes, and start again. The turban will have an influence on our minds, actions and attitudes, if we allow it.

Whilst it is right that we are to put off sin, and the old man, we have become so legalistic in the Church today that some sins are definitely considered worse than others. Telling lies for your boss does not compare with murder; but in this we are quite wrong. We have to understand because God is so holy, anything remotely connected with sin will not pass near His holiness, and with Him there are no degrees of sin.

The servant's heart in this instance cries out to God to be set free from the slavery of sin, but also needs to understand that the manifold grace which God gives does cover personal sins. We all have insecurities and imbalances in our lives, some of which result in sin, and others which result in bondages that inhibit us. Either way, we have to give these areas to the Lord, that He might continue the good work He has begun in us, and present us faultless before the throne of God (Jude 1:24-25).

Sin cannot enter into the presence of our Holy God, and we have to be clean from all unrighteousness before we may enter the throne room of grace. The Holy Spirit leads us and convicts us of sin in our lives; not sin that is unforgiven but rather areas in our lives that do not measure up to God's standard, and it becomes a decision of our will whether or not we submit to the leading of the Holy Spirit and begin the process of change.

The servant's heart, with regards to other people and their sin, should exhibit an understanding of the dilemma which most people encounter when their lives are not right with the Lord, or the servant's heart, in its attitude to the sin of others, should display an understanding of the struggle all believers face in seeking to live right before God, and the dilemma which results when their lives are not right with the Lord. The servant's heart is to love the person, not the sin; to compliment the believer on his faithfulness, and to gently encourage whatever changes the Holy Spirit is unctioning. At times when there is a sin which binds an individual, it is important to encourage the person to be open with the Lord and repent hourly if necessary – eventually it will become every hour and a half, and following on, then the growth will begin to show. Jericho was walked around for seven days before the walls fell!

We should not allow the believer to fall away from his sanctification because he is still too weak to resist temptation. We know that all temptation comes with a way out; but some of us, at the onset of temptation, do not see the way out, nor the ensuing victory (1 Corinthians 10:13). At all costs, the servant's heart must maintain the conviction that the sinner has already been forgiven; even before victory is reached.

CHRIST—among us but separate from us
    Isaiah 7:14; Matthew 1:23
        He Didn't Forget Who He Was

For six years Joseph Pistone lived among Mafia families as an FBI undercover agent. During that time he had to feign a personal interest in the Mafia's monstrous social schemes: thievery, murder, extortion, and drug dealings. He had to produce funds for his capo (provided by the FBI through unclaimed stolen property) and had to lie for a high moral purpose—to enable the United States government to severely damage organized crime in America. From that horrifying nightmare he emerged unaltered; his personality, values, and attention to physical conditioning were intact. When his superiors finally pulled him off the job, he had no trouble leaving the role of Donnie Brasco.

Jesus came undercover to our fallen world. He stayed plenty long enough to forget why he came—but he didn't. He identified so strongly with us that he could have seen our sins as harmless pranks—but he didn't. He could have become so much a part of us as to forget who he was—but he didn't. Pistone's lifestyle said "I'll become like you." Jesus' lifestyle said "I won't become like you; I'll let everyone of you become like me."[88]

Having said all the above with regards to sin, we must never ever forget the power of grace. To a sinner, we **must** preach the gospel in such a way that it gives people 'licence to sin', then we have preached theGrace to its fullest. That is the point of the Gospel. there is nothing anyone of us could do that would make us unacceptable to God. Whilst in our quest to fulfil the destiny God has in store for each of us, we will encounter issues, situations and people that have us tread close to, or over, the boundaries we have set for ourselves. If we begin to see that hthese boundaries have been set by opurselves, we can understand how easily we fall back under the Law, then we can begin to understand the manifest grace that abounds to each of us. In ALL things, rest assured that grace abounds much **more** where sin is.

CHAPTER 3
WHY DO WE NEED A SERVANT'S HEART?

Cain did not have a Servant's Heart, and it showed in his offering which was unacceptable to God.

Genesis 4:4-5,

⁴ Abel also brought of the firstborn of his flock and of their fat. And the Lord respected Abel and his offering, ⁵ but He did not respect Cain and his offering. And Cain was very angry, and his countenance fell.[89]

Cain was under the impression that the offering which he made by his own wisdom would be good enough for God, and that he did not need to follow the example to his family set by God. This led to Cain becoming jealous and the resultant murder of Abel.

When we do not have a servant's heart, we tend to try and please God with actions which we deem necessary, whether God has asked for them or not. We further rationalise that, should we think up a better plan than the one God gave us, then why not use that one?

God gave us His plans because He expects us to relaise that we are not above Him.

Isaiah 55:8,

⁸ "For My thoughts *are* not your thoughts,
Nor *are* your ways My ways," says the Lord.[90]

God's reason for expecting us to follow the types and shadows which He placed throughout Scripture is that we may continue in fellowship with Him, and remain on track as regards His desires for our lives.

We do not have to go to a fortune-teller to find out what God desires; we have His living Word to speak to us, to enlighten situations through the working of the Holy Spirit. To avoid seeking God in this manner means that we consider ourselves, as 21st-Century individuals, as being above a book written four thousand years ago.

We cannot expect to understand the command of pick up our cross and follow Jesus if we are still the almighty "I" ourselves. When we rely on our own intellect and assume the role of the Holy Spirit in our own lives, we generally make a mess. We need to submit to the leadership of the Holy Trinity.

Unfortunately, we are now in a dispensation that declares that man is all powerful, that minds have reached perfection, that man and women have equal rights, that man is a superior being, and that the world would not existed beyoond the year 2000, had Bill Gates did not fix the Y2K bug!

Surprise, surprise; we are well into the new millennium, bugs and all; and only God did not change, neither upgrade His programming to be Y2K compliant, or even blink as the clock struck 12 on December 31, 1999.

All of the above shows how self-reliant and self-dependant we have become, and this from beings that cannot prevent anything happening which is ordained by God. We do not stop to even associate God with healing, because the doctors have medicine; food is not associated with the miracle of creation, (unless I am cooking!) but is only available because of the advantages of green houses! Rubbish! We need to begin to realise we serve a God that holds us in the palm of His hands, who holds the world together by His words. We do not run the watering system of the earth, or Ethiopia would have rain; we do not have access to the earthquake timetable. We daren't assume that we can control the weather and seasons.

With the kind of mindset imparted into each one of us growing up in this computerised age, God cannot break through our senses unless He first breaks the shells we have made, and reveals us to ourselves as we really are. God truly is holy, and we have no concept of holiness nowadays, because we don't know what holy is. We know what it should be, but do not have a revelation unless the Holy Spirit gives us one.

You cannot pretend to have a servant's heart. It is a gift from God; made available to us as He mends the creation that satan has fowled up.

We can experience glimpses of Heaven, glimpses of God's presence, visions of God and Heaven, but until we experience the depth of the sin we are in, the level of filth that we contain, the abhorrence of God towards sin, we will never be able to lay down everything for God. Unless we have a sincere revelation of sin, its consequences and its costs, we will never truly appreciate the gift of salvation; the cost Jesus paid to lay down His life for us.

It is only after we have experienced the cleansing of Jesus as we stand before Him and confess our sins, and realise our need to change radically to be able to serve Him as He desires, that the servant's heart can begin to be formed in us.

This experience is a process different to the experience of salvation, because the person who accepts salvation is usually unaware of the depth of sin, and of the depth of the calling that will be placed on his life. The Holy Spirit will reveal again and again, during our walk with Him, areas in our lives that need the cleansing power of the Blood of Jesus.

CHAPTER 4
HOW DO WE RECEIVE A SERVANT'S HEART?

Most of us reach a stage in our Christian walk where we realise we have outgrown the fairy tales and now need to see some of God's power in action today. This can be as a result of many things in our lives, but more than likely the Holy Spirit decides to encourage us onto new heights in Him and as a result we have the furnace turned up in our lives. The only way to purify gold is to heat the gold until all the junk, or dross, as it is correctly called, bubbles to the surface and is then gently poured off the top of the container that now contains pure gold.

Sounds great in theory; but like most object lessons, the actual work in our lives is often painful, and can become embarrassing as we realise we still have remnants of the old man which have been lying comatose but not dead. Be aware, of course, that the Holy Spirit is not the only one who will be active during this time of releasing the dross. Satan will do his utmost to bombard you with all sorts of junk that you never ever had problems with before, in an effort to discourage and falsely condemn you during this time. Be of good cheer and courage as you stand firm in your armour, and know you are covered under the Blood of Jesus Christ; your sins are forgiven, and you are more than a conqueror.

Jesus does not allow us to go through these trials and refining times to harm us or to see us trip up and fall flat on our noses. He allows us to undergo these experiences because He sees us in all the wonder and glory of the creation we were meant to be, without the flaws of sin, and because of this, He encourages us to be the best us we can be!

As we undergo the refining process we will see a change in our circumstances. This can involve a change in job, a loss of something that is dearer to us than Christ is, a removal of old habits and the instilling of some new ones, strife in your home environment, financial tests, health tests, emotional and relationship challenges, (sometimes involving those you thought would support you through anything), a change in your vision, (possibly even the death of your vision), and many other "gentle" challenges.

Once we understand that we need the servant's heart in order to be able to serve the Lord with our all, we will have to crucify everything in our lives which does not conform to this goal. It will be a decision that will drastically change our life - be careful what you are asking for, you will get it. Be prepared to take the challenge head on, and be aware of the spiritual war in which you will be engaged. Remember, Jesus said that whatever we ask, we will receive - He was referring to spiritual growth as well.

As we submit to the leading of the Holy Spirit in our lives, He will convict of sin and hard areas in our lives; areas where our own best interests have been at the centre of our hearts.

Repentance is an important aspect of the change to a servant's heart, as the Holy Spirit shows us what we are, and then illuminates what we should be. Repentance is a complete turn around and walking in a completely opposite direction.

This is usually a period of deep introspection as the Holy Spirit leads us to separate ourselves from the world around us, and to spend time in the presence of the Lord, the one who understands the depths of our hearts, and searches deep within them to reveal the areas that do not bring Him glory.

During this period in my own life, I experienced a vision of a house that was spotless. A sort of video-camera tour through the house occurred, looking into all the areas a woman would look for cobwebs and dust, and finding none. I felt extremely pleased with the cleanliness of the house and was then taken into the cellar of the house! Here the cobwebs abounded in areas where the house was not open to the public view; hidden beneath the plush carpets and fancy furniture.

Many of our hearts are like this - on the top we look like really on-top-of-everything Christians, but underneath are issues we are not cleaning up in our lives - secret sins that the Father knows of, and wants us to be cleansed of. One of the most important things we need to realise and receive a revelation of at this time, is that no matter what we are struggling with as far as sin goes in our lives, God is and remains faithful to us. I have learnt over the past years that there are times when I fall on my nose for the same thing, and as I stand up, admit my failure, and genuinely desire to see God glorified in my life, it is the fact that I stand up again and not giving in that counts. The giving in refers to walking away from God because I have failed and do not forgive myself. God expects me to come to Him immediately - even ten seconds - after falling, admit the failure, and stand washed and ready to move on to victory – it doesn't matter that you don't know how to get out of the situation; the fact that you are willing to allow God to change you and your circumstances is what matters.

The Lord is extremely gentle with us during these times; allowing Scriptures to encourage us as we find that we are all alone at the brook of Kidron, and sometimes feel we have no contact with the outside world. We are fed by the Lord during this time, as friends and relatives withdraw during the separation period - usually because we are undergoing changes that make them realise that we are serious with the Lord, but they do not have the commitment to undergo this level of surgery themselves. Be at peace with them, and allow the Lord to give you new friends and family that have been through the experiences you are about to face, because the Lord will never set you in a position without help and encouragement.

The other important aspect to remember about this period of sitting alone is that you asked for it! There will be times when like Elijah, who prayed for no rain, and then went to the Brook of Kidron, and when the brook dried up because of no rain, suddenly questions whether God was even there or not. What more proof could he have needed than the fact that he too was experiencing the effects of the drought? Sometimes it becomes necessary for us to spend time evaluating the prayers we are so glib to pray and check the circumstances we are in, and find out whether we originally asked for the situation.

You may find there is only one person you can compare notes with, but trust in the Lord who has begun the good work in you to complete His work, and also to draw the others you have left behind, at their own pace. Never force your spiritual experiences onto another person - we are unique and all need to change as the Lord leads us, and not as the Lord led another. I may fight with a revelation for six months you snapped up one morning in your muesli, but you may not experience another revelation I need in my life.

As the Lord changes our hearts some of us, due to our upbringing and circumstances will need to learn to cry; others, to laugh; some, to accept responsibility; and still others, to lay down burdens not theirs to carry. There will be the temptation to run away from all the testing and changes happening in your heart; but, like Much Afraid in the Book 'Hinds Feet in High Places', we must ask the Saviour to bind us to the altar so that we do not run away. It is at times like this you realise exactly how fickle the human heart is; for as we really and truly desire to change towards the vision that Christ has of us, as soon as the going gets tough, the instinct is to run away.

There were times in my own life when enough was enough, and having no one else to talk too at 10 O'clock at night all on my own, the walls of the room would begin to close in, and I would find all sorts of gremlins coming to destroy and rob me of any level of sanctification I thought was possible. It was at these times I would cry to the Lord and express I was really hurting; that I felt that I couldn't go on, and this was too much for me. Those were the times when the gentleness of the Lord would become evident; where He would either send peace that would stop the sobs and send me to sleep with the comfort of His arms around me, or He would remind me of a verse or promise that He had given me, or, sometimes, even just allow me to admit that I was not coping, and having admitted that, allow me to decide whether or not I would continue, no matter what changed or what did not. (I think that a level of stubbornness prevailed many a time when I thought I was pinned to the ground.)

Allow the Lord time to change you - do not expect to receive the servant's heart after one howling session. It took however many years to build those walls and fortresses, you will be too vulnerable without them. The Lord will lead us with gentleness and firmness; not remove all our clothing and throw us into a snowstorm.

Ezekiel 36:26-27,

^{26} I will give you a new heart and put a new spirit within you; I will take the heart of stone out of your flesh and give you a heart of flesh. ^{27} I will put My Spirit within you and cause you to walk in My statutes, and you will keep My judgments and do *them*. [91]

The above passage explains what happens when we receive the servant's heart. The Lord takes away our heart of stone, and gives us a heart of flesh. This heart transplant is usually done without anaesthetic! We are allowed to feel the pain of having our heart wrenched out, and the gasping as the new one is inserted. The Lord determines the time of the transplant, but we are aware long before the operation we have a faulty heart at work, the same as actual heart patients are aware.

When we receive our new hearts, we also receive a new level of awareness of God's Spirit in us, which causes us to follow in the statutes and judgements of the Lord. We will no longer fight the good fight on our own miserable strength, but will fight in the resurrection power of Jesus Christ.

Once we have received our new hearts, this is not the end of the road. These soft, pliable, gentle and loving hearts have to be kept that way, and God does not use fabric conditioner. He uses a grater that grates off the hard parts we allow there, and the fresh bleeding brings life to the dead areas that grow around our hearts again and again. As our hearts are held against the grater, God squeezes these spiritual organs; a feeling we come to know and appreciate for its firmness, but also receive with conviction, as we realise again that God has shown us an area in our life we need to work on.

The following testimony is taken by Keith Green from the autobiography of Rees Howell, written by Norman Grubb, and describes Rees Howell's heart changing experience:

The meeting with the Holy Ghost was just as real to [Howells] as his [conversion to Christianity] three years before. 'I saw him as a person apart from the flesh and blood and He said to me, "As the Saviour had a body, so I dwell in the cleansed temple of the believer. I am God and I come to ask you to give your body to me, *that I may work through you. I need a body for my temple.*

But it must belong to me without reserve for two persons with different wills can never live in the same body. Will you give me yours? You must go out. I shall not mix myself with yourself."I saw the honour He gave me in offering to indwell me but there were many things very dear to me and I knew that He wouldn't keep even one of them. The change He would make was very clear. It meant that every bit of my fallen nature was to go to the cross and He would bring His own life and His own nature into *me. It was unconditional surrender.*

The story continues with God giving Howells an ultimatum: would he obey or not? He had to give God his reply the following week.

For the next few days Howell wept continually. He couldn't eat or sleep and lost seven pounds. This was the hardest decision he would ever have to make – to hand over his life like a blank cheque to God. Was he willing to let go of all his dreams, all his *possessions, and let the Holy Spirit take full control?*

This is what happened when he reached his decision:

'*Nothing was more real to me than the process I went through* that whole week… The Holy Spirit went on dealing with me exposing the root of my nature which was self and you can only get out of a thing what is in its root. Sin was cancelled and it wasn't sin He was dealing with; it was self – that thing which came from the Fall. He was not going to take any superficial surrender. He put His finger on each part of my self-life, and I had to decide in cold blood. He could never take a thing away until I *gave my consent.*'

Like the Apostle Paul, Howells found God does not want us to play games. There comes a time when the Holy Spirit puts His finger on areas in our lives and asks us to hand over control of them to Him. In order to receive the resurrection life and the power that goes along with it, we must be willing to let go of everything we hold close. Sometimes our flesh screams as we do this. Other times it devises subtle ways of getting us off-track. Instead of kicking and screaming, our flesh quietly tries to distract us with side issues – anything to keep us from giving everything *to God.*'[92]

CHAPTER 5
WHAT IS THE CURRENT TREND OF TODAY'S CHRISTIAN WITH REGARDS TO THE NECESSITY OF A SERVANT'S HEART?

Research carried out for the purpose of this study showed that, whilst many Christians were unaware of the actual term, servant's heart, most Christians after a few minutes reflection, could give a degree of knowledge concerning what they felt the term should mean (this included the functioning of the Fruit of the Spirit, as mentioned in Galatians 5:22-23), as well as being able to describe which attributes the servant's heart should be devoid of.

It appears that, as with most humans, Christians are able to tell others what should and should not be done in the Christian walk, but are not themselves always walking in the victory they claim is available.

Whilst the concept of a servant's heart is understood, many Christians are not putting this into practice. This can be the result of laziness on behalf of the Christian, apathy, bad teaching, incorrect doctrines, and any other term we could wish to use to cover the complacency rampant in the Church today.

When questioned as to the reason for the apathy in regards to the process of change in their hearts, a common complaint was a lack of motivation. It seems this ideal given to us by Paul of being able to live holy lives, has become an ideal beyond the reach of the average Christian today. The motivation required to stand and be counted holy before the Lord, has been replaced with the ability to stand washed in God's grace, and rather than attain the crowns we are promised, we settle for sliding into Heaven by grace.

This kind of apathy has crept into the entire world society and shows in the way the families are being run. Children are left with people who do not necessarily have the same spiritual and moral discernment of the family, and this is contributing towards both a spiritual and moral decay in today's society.

Whilst some of the research shows that the questionnaire raised questions in peoples' hearts, it remains to be seen how much of this questionnaire will actually become a reality in the lives of the people who answered it. It is one thing to acknowledge there is room for improvement, but it is another to cold-bloodedly initiate the process of change on your own. No, we are not suggesting works, but the idea of moving closer to God by an act of our wills which will enable God to move closer to us.

As part of the research project, I asked a group of Christians 20 questions concerning the servant's heart. The questions were designed in such a way as to encourage the participants to equate the term with Biblical characters, to evaluate their own personal lives currently, and to decide on their own, how much the questions had stirred their hearts towards change.

Whilst some of the people had experienced heart changes, the fruit of those hearts being soft now, might not be apparent, and this hopefully led to a renewed commitment in their lives.

One of the most beautiful characteristics of the Lord is His graciousness to allow us to start again when we have fallen. When we fall short in our own capacities, He is ready to pick us up and set us on our feet again.

As with most Christians, when placed in a fix, the idea of sacrificing everything to Jesus becomes glorious. The practical implications, however, leave many wounded on the sidelines. When confronted with the ideas of loosing family, friends, jobs, possessions, once the process begins, the sacrifice seems to loose the ideals it was supposed to represent.
Perhaps the fact so many give up on the way, is the reason this kind of dedication is seen so rarely in our times.

I know for myself that even now, years after being asked what I would give up for the power of God to be manifest in my life, and answering 'everything', there are days when the apparent mess my life is in at the moment makes it seem as though there is no way that this could be the beginning of the manifestation of the power of God.

However having made the decision and seeing how all things in my life seemed to be turned upside down, yet I still desire the power of God to be manifest through my life.

There have been days when I have asked the Lord to leave me alone for ten minutes so I can lick my wounds, but He is always there when I am ready to continue the fight. Some of the circumstances I have experienced are the results of bad decisions, and others are the results of deciding Jesus Christ had to come first in my life. The latter resulted in a time of reassessing various areas of my life and stating that there were to be no more compromises. It is amazing how, when we decide to stand for Jesus, satan makes sure you are standing on a rug - one he has no qualms pulling out from under your feet.

One of the hardest things to occur in your life during this time of shaking, is knowing what was is a result of your mistakes and what is from God. We are sometimes warned that times of shaking are coming so we can put our trust in our Father. The difficult part comes in accepting your mistakes, confessing them to God and allowing Him to change the mess you have made when you thought that you were doing His Will.

One of the most prominent problems in the Church today is the 'Come to Jesus and all is forgiven and life becomes Heaven on Earth' theory. This leads many into a relationship with Christ where they think everything will go well for them, especially if they are already destitute and hanging on to sanity by a thread. We are failing to teach these people that only then does the fight start, and subsequently, as soon as all hell is let loose, then they fade and disappear.

When new converts are taught the meaning of the term 'servant's heart', what it entails, and how their lives will have to change, Christianity becomes a challenge, not a wishy-washy type of doctrine and fairytale, - even though we will all live happily ever after.

CHAPTER 6
BIBLICAL EXAMPLES OF PEOPLE WITH SERVANTS HEARTS.

Having discussed the various principles to do with the servant's heart, some practical examples are required to draw attention to the people depicting these attributes in the Bible. We will look into the lives of certain biblical characters and learn from their examples.

ESTHER
Esther has two particularly well-known quotations, viz. "If I perish, I perish", and "Who knows but that you were put here for a time such as this".

Mordecai, Esther's guardian, is a symbol of the Holy Spirit in the life of the believer; the one who sees the wickedness of Haman (depicting satan) and encourages Esther(depicting the believer) to remove the evil one from power, under the direction of the Holy Spirit's leading.

Esther had managed to land on her feet after being orphaned at an early age. She was of Jewish descent, particularly lovely to look at, and had won the heart of the king to such a degree that she replaced the deposed Queen Vashti. Not bad for an orphan!

Mordecai, her adoptive parent, taught Esther all the customs and practices of the Jewish religion, but advised her to keep her genealogy quiet. The proverb, 'train a child in the way he should go and when he is grown he will not depart from it' (Proverbs 22:6), shows true with Esther's life.

As Queen, Esther was in the position to totally ignore the plight of the locals, and turn her head away; akin to the time of the French Revolution, when Marie Antoinette told the locals that if they did not have bread they should eat cake.

Esther was completely aware of her background, remained humble in spite of her social elevation, and still maintained a level of compassion for others.

Esther put aside her own self-interest by approaching the king without an invitation. Esther knew she could face death without a hearing for entering the inner court without an appointment; but, realising God was in control, she approached the king. This abandonment of her own personal safety gave way for the Holy Spirit to remove the wickedness in the palace and replace evil counsel with good counsel.

Esther depicts the servant's heart by her expressed compassion, her willingness to physically put her own life in danger for another, her subjection of her body to a period of fasting for the plight of others, and also by revealing her own past, which could have had a detrimental effect on her marriage.

Esther stepped over the line of dying to self, when she voiced the eternal words, 'If I perish, I perish.' Esther was prepared to give her life for the safety of others.

RUTH

As a person that characterise the servant's heart go, possibly none were so eloquent as that of Ruth to her mother-in-law Naomi.

Ruth 1:16-17,

> [16] But Ruth said:
>
> "Entreat me not to leave you,
> *Or to* turn back from following after you;
> For wherever you go, I will go;
> And wherever you lodge, I will lodge;
> Your people *shall be* my people,
> And your God, my God.
>
> [17] Where you die, I will die,
> And there will I be buried.
> The Lord do so to me, and more also,
> If *anything but* death parts you and me."[93]

Ruth here vocalises the essesnce of the servant's heart, by showing her complete denial od self, and the unconditional following of Naomi. This self-denial led Ruth to following Naomi's commands, that eventually led to Ruth's marriage to Boaz.

We can all surmise what might have happened had Ruth not submitted to Naomi - there could have been an entirely different genealogy to the birth of King David, had he still been born, and also of Jesus Christ.

We need to understand what Ruth did not have insightinto during her time of testing and character building. Ruth could easily have given up during those difficult months. Instead, she showed herself faithful to the most menial of tasks, showed herself reliable and steadfast when presented with less-than-perfect circumstances, and remained humble instead of allowing herself to become hard of heart because of her circumstances.

We have to be aware that Ruth was a Moabitess, a nation that was despised by the Israelites. Ruth would already have stood judged, in a sense, before she set foot in Israel, but her loyalty to her new family and God set her apart from any other person in God's eyes.

The one seeking a servant's heart can learn from Ruth's complete submission, and also from her attitude. Submission, in the servant's heart is not quietly accepting anything, but is a decision to be led in truth by the Holy Spirit.

Perhaps the hardest prayer for a servant's heart would be to be able to pray the same words that Ruth spoke to Naomi; to be able to offer one's life to the Lord with the same abandonment as Ruth offered herself into Naomi's hands.

ELISHA
Elisha was a young man of purpose, a man who sought the double portion of blessing from his master Elijah. Elisha showed himself to be hard working, loyal and steadfast. Elisha served under Elijah for many years as his servant. Elisha was obviously from a wealthy family as he left a field where he was ploughing with 12 yoke of oxen. 2 Kings 3:11 quotes Elisha as being known as the one who poured water on the prophet Elijah's hands. How would we handle that kind of reputation today?

Elisha knew the value of servanthood, and this enabled him to receive the double portion of the blessing he desired. Elisha stayed with Elijah, his spiritual father, after he had learnt all of what Elijah could teach him, but Elisha never outgrew his need of his teacher. Too many people consider themselves above their teachers, and fall into traps set after this pride has reared its head.

Elisha was only allowed to receive the double portion if he witnessed Elijah being taken into Heaven - this meant a constant vigilance on behalf of Elisha. Should we not also be constantly in this state of anxious awareness of the return of our Lord, or have we, like Elijah's other disciples, learnt to stand back and watch from afar?

Elisha depicts the servant's heart in the vigilance he displayed regarding Elijah. Elisha never wavered in his service to Elijah.

THE SERVANT KING
Isaiah 42:1-9,
>"Behold! My Servant whom I uphold,
>My Elect One *in whom* My soul delights!
>I have put My Spirit upon Him;
>He will bring forth justice to the Gentiles.
>
>² He will not cry out, nor raise *His voice,*
>Nor cause His voice to be heard in the street.
>
>³ A bruised reed He will not break,
>And smoking flax He will not quench;
>He will bring forth justice for truth.
>
>⁴ He will not fail nor be discouraged,
>Till He has established justice in the earth;
>And the coastlands shall wait for His law."
>
>⁵ Thus says God the Lord,
>Who created the heavens and stretched them out,
>Who spread forth the earth and that which comes from it,
>Who gives breath to the people on it,
>And spirit to those who walk on it:
>
>⁶ "I, the Lord, have called You in righteousness,
>And will hold Your hand;
>I will keep You and give You as a covenant to the people,
>As a light to the Gentiles,

> [7] To open blind eyes,
> To bring out prisoners from the prison,
> Those who sit in darkness from the prison house.
>
> [8] I *am* the Lord, that *is* My name;
> And My glory I will not give to another,
> Nor My praise to carved images.
>
> [9] Behold, the former things have come to pass,
> And new things I declare;
> Before they spring forth I tell you of them."[94]

Isaiah 49:1-9,
> "Listen, O coastlands, to Me,
> And take heed, you peoples from afar!
> The Lord has called Me from the womb;
> From the matrix of My mother He has made mention of My name.
>
> [2] And He has made My mouth like a sharp sword;
> In the shadow of His hand He has hidden Me,
> And made Me a polished shaft;
> In His quiver He has hidden Me."
>
> [3] "And He said to me,
> 'You *are* My servant, O Israel,
> In whom I will be glorified.'
>
> [4] Then I said, 'I have labored in vain,
> I have spent my strength for nothing and in vain;
> Yet surely my just reward *is* with the Lord,
> And my work with my God.' "
>
> [5] "And now the Lord says,
> Who formed Me from the womb *to be* His Servant,
> To bring Jacob back to Him,
> So that Israel is gathered to Him
> (For I shall be glorious in the eyes of the Lord,
> And My God shall be My strength),
>
> [6] Indeed He says,
> 'It is too small a thing that You should be My Servant
> To raise up the tribes of Jacob,
> And to restore the preserved ones of Israel;
> I will also give You as a light to the Gentiles,
> That You should be My salvation to the ends of the earth.' "
>
> [7] Thus says the Lord,
> The Redeemer of Israel, their Holy One,
> To Him whom man despises,
> To Him whom the nation abhors,
> To the Servant of rulers:
> "Kings shall see and arise,
> Princes also shall worship,

The Servant's Heart

Because of the Lord who is faithful,
The Holy One of Israel;
And He has chosen You."

[8] Thus says the Lord:
"In an acceptable time I have heard You,
And in the day of salvation I have helped You;
I will preserve You and give You
As a covenant to the people,
To restore the earth,
To cause them to inherit the desolate heritages;

[9] That You may say to the prisoners, 'Go forth,'
To those who *are* in darkness, 'Show yourselves.'
"They shall feed along the roads,
And their pastures *shall be* on all desolate heights.[95]

Isaiah 50:4-11,

[4] "The Lord God has given Me
The tongue of the learned,
That I should know how to speak
A word in season to *him who is* weary.
He awakens Me morning by morning,
He awakens My ear
To hear as the learned.

[5] The Lord God has opened My ear;
And I was not rebellious,
Nor did I turn away.

[6] I gave My back to those who struck *Me*,
And My cheeks to those who plucked out the beard;
I did not hide My face from shame and spitting.

[7] "For the Lord God will help Me;
Therefore I will not be disgraced;
Therefore I have set My face like a flint,
And I know that I will not be ashamed.

[8] *He is* near who justifies Me;
Who will contend with Me?
Let us stand together.
Who *is* My adversary?
Let him come near Me.

[9] Surely the Lord God will help Me;
Who *is* he *who* will condemn Me?
Indeed they will all grow old like a garment;
The moth will eat them up.

[10] "Who among you fears the Lord?
Who obeys the voice of His Servant?
Who walks in darkness

And has no light?
Let him trust in the name of the Lord
And rely upon his God.

[11] Look, all you who kindle a fire,
Who encircle *yourselves* with sparks:
Walk in the light of your fire and in the sparks you have kindled—
This you shall have from My hand:
You shall lie down in torment.[96]

Isaiah 52:13 – 53:12,

[13] Behold, My Servant shall deal prudently;
He shall be exalted and extolled and be very high.

[14] Just as many were astonished at you,
So His visage was marred more than any man,
And His form more than the sons of men;

[15] So shall He sprinkle many nations.
Kings shall shut their mouths at Him;
For what had not been told them they shall see,
And what they had not heard they shall consider.
Who has believed our report?
And to whom has the arm of the Lord been revealed?

[2] For He shall grow up before Him as a tender plant,
And as a root out of dry ground.
He has no form or comeliness;
And when we see Him,
There is no beauty that we should desire Him.

[3] He is despised and rejected by men,
A Man of sorrows and acquainted with grief.
And we hid, as it were, *our* faces from Him;
He was despised, and we did not esteem Him.

[4] Surely He has borne our griefs
And carried our sorrows;
Yet we esteemed Him stricken,
Smitten by God, and afflicted.

[5] But He *was* wounded for our transgressions,
He was bruised for our iniquities;
The chastisement for our peace *was* upon Him,
And by His stripes we are healed.

[6] All we like sheep have gone astray;
We have turned, every one, to his own way;
And the Lord has laid on Him the iniquity of us all.

[7] He was oppressed and He was afflicted,
Yet He opened not His mouth;
He was led as a lamb to the slaughter,
And as a sheep before its shearers is silent,

The Servant's Heart

So He opened not His mouth.

⁸ He was taken from prison and from judgment,
And who will declare His generation?
For He was cut off from the land of the living;
For the transgressions of My people He was stricken.

⁹ And they made His grave with the wicked—
But with the rich at His death,
Because He had done no violence,
Nor *was any* deceit in His mouth.

¹⁰ Yet it pleased the Lord to bruise Him;
He has put *Him* to grief.
When You make His soul an offering for sin,
He shall see *His* seed, He shall prolong *His* days,
And the pleasure of the Lord shall prosper in His hand.

¹¹ He shall see the labor of His soul, *and* be satisfied.
By His knowledge My righteous Servant shall justify many,
For He shall bear their iniquities.

¹² Therefore I will divide Him a portion with the great,
And He shall divide the spoil with the strong,
Because He poured out His soul unto death,
And He was numbered with the transgressors,
And He bore the sin of many,
And made intercession for the transgressors.[97]

These passages are known as 'the Servant Songs', and are taken from the Book of Isaiah. Whilst they are all referring to the Messiah and His attributes, these Scriptures are a barometer for each one of us. These passages are a prophetic description of how Jesus Christ would respond to the injustices done to Him. They also show His compassion where Jesus sees someone who is floundering in their faith. The calling to set the captives free and open blind eyes is an instruction to each one of us today.

We cannot, however, expect to use the power of God available unless we have submitted ourselves to completely doing his will. Our God remains a jealous God, and will not share His honour and glory, nor compete with our pride and conceit.

MARY
Luke 1:38,

³⁸ Then Mary said, "Behold the maidservant of the Lord! Let it be to me according to your word." And the angel departed from her.[98]

The famous words of Mary to the angel when told of her impending pregnancy with our Lord Jesus Christ echo down through the ages, instilling in each one of us the attributes of a servant's heart. Mary was a betrothed virgin, which meant that she was spoken for, that Joseph had already accepted her to be his wife. Mary was not in a community that accepted promiscuity as today's society does, and she could have been stoned if the community found out about her pregnancy.

Mary accepted what the angel of the Lord told her, and we see later that a characteristic of hers was to ponder things in her heart. Mary knew God was in control and He would sort out her reputation and circumstances. We see that an angel of the Lord spoke to Joseph concerning the pregnancy, Mary did not go and report her experience to everyone, but remained patient for the Lord's timing.

ABIGAIL
When we take a look at Abigail (1 Samuel 25:2-44), we see a really intelligent lady, who had the right ideas concerning her submissive attitude and respect for her husband. She was married to a man, Nabal, whose name meant fool or scoundrel. This man had met some of David's men, and refused to offer them shelter and food even after David's men had protected Nabal's shepherds. David reacted by girding up his army for war against Nabal and his family.

When Abigail heard about the situation, she immediately assessed whether she should go behind her husband's back and save his life, or if she should remain at home and await her own death. She chose to take the matter into her own hands and collected a meal for David and his men, which she delivered herself and also apologised on behalf of Nabal, asking that Nabal's sin fall on her head rather than on his own. David accepted the meal and blessed Abigail for her bravery. Abigail here showed herself as a shadow or type of Jesus Christ, who saw the punishment to be metered out for Nabal's folly and intervened at the possible cost of her own life. This also shows that Abigail loved her husband even though he was a scoundrel and a fool. She was willing to lay down her life for him.

Abigail showed her servant's heart by trying to make amends for her husband's stupidity and callousness. She was prepared to place herself in front of David, and open herself up to his anger. David could have metered out Nabal's punishment on Abigail if he had wanted to. Abigail also opened herself up to the anger of her husband when he found out that she had deliberately fed David's men after he had forbidden the act. Abigail also shows us how wives are to respond when placed in an area of possible sin by unbelieving spouses, we are to approach the King, and He will protect us.

Abigail's reward for the meal was a blessing, and when her husband died because of the hardness of his own heart, Abigail was made David's wife. The Bible refers to Nabal's heart as turning to stone inside him. Abigail showed sensitivity, wisdom, and insight in this situation. She managed to serve David without being malicious to her husband, without blaming him, without condemning him.

PAUL
Paul had possibly the most dramatic change of heart recorded in Scripture. Paul was intent on wiping the memory of Jesus Christ from the face of the planet, and set about doing so. When Paul was on the road to Damascus and met Jesus Christ, the resultant heart change altered a man who persecuted Christians into one of the most well known Christians through all the centuries to follow.

Paul suffered all sorts of injustices in line with those he inflicted on others previously. He suffered rejection by the original disciples, who thought he was setting traps for them; was beaten by his own citizens; was jailed, stoned, and shipwrecked, and then chained to a Roman guard for many years.

In all these things Paul remained positive, and spent his life teaching and writing to the new Churches the doctrines we still abide by today. Paul's life-changing change of heart gave him the strength to continue on his course, to run and complete the race set before him. Another thing to note about Paul is that once he stood up and set his face towards Jesus Christ, there is no mention of him running himself down for the things he did in his past, Paul knew total forgiveness for his sins and continued without looking back – something we all need a revelation on I think.

VIRGIN TO DIE FOR FATHER'S OATH
This is a prime example of watching what you promise the Lord in a time of fear. Jephthah decided he would offer whatever came out of his house first to the Lord if he returned victorious from a war with the Ammonites (Judges 11). The man's only daughter ran out to meet him. The child asked for two months to mourn before accepting her fate, which the father allowed. She showed no sign of rebellion, malice, disobedience, anger or any of the other possible emotions. She accepted her father had made a decision and a vow to God and was prepared to follow his decisions.

We probably cannot imagine what went through the child's mind as she waited for two months to die. Probably only those on death row would understand. There is no record of discussions to find loopholes in the law or the scriptures to change the situation, both parties realised an oath had been sworn to Almighty God and both had enough respect for this oath to complete the deal.

Having made the oath, the father submitted to the consequences. He too, had a two month period of waiting before he had to complete his part of the oath, and had to face the loss of his only child, knowing he would be responsible for her death. So many of us would back out of that kind of commitment to the Lord, especially if we could say that God is a God of Love and would not expect the father to fulfil his oath. The father became a type or shadow of God the Father when He had to watch man mess up the earth, knowing eventually when the time was completed, He would send His only Son to die.

HANNAH
Hannah depicts the servant's heart by acknowledging in the the vow she made, that the life of the child she had so desperately wanted would be given up. Hannah was accused by Eli the High Priest of being drunk and muttering in the Temple. Instead of becoming angry at this accusation, Hannah related her story to Eli, and then parted with Eli's blessing. True enough, Hannah's prayers were answered, and after weaning the child, she handed Samuel over to Eli to remain in the Temple for the rest of his life.

Hannah continued to see the child once a year when she would return to the Temple with clothes for the child. We read that Hannah had other children.It is apparent that because her heart attitude had been right, she was prepared to sacrifice that which she loved the most, so God would receive glory and honour. No doubt Hannah never stopped loving Samuel, but we see how faithful God is to return and restore to us more than we have originally lost. Especially when we loose so that God can gain.

Hannah might have had to hand over the upbringing of her child to another person, but her faith in God remained steadfast as she sewed clothes for the child each year and visited him. We especially see Hannah's faith in God in light of the fact that Eli's two sons, Hophni and Phineas, were renown for their antics with the ladies, and their demands that changed the sacrifices to God, and the way that the portions for the High Priests were given. Hannah had given her child to be brought up in the Temple to the father of these same two delinquent children. If he had failed with his own children, Hannah had to trust God He would not fail with Samuel.

We see Hannah did not harbour bitterness or anger towards God because she made the vow to give Samuel back. Had she done this, we can suppose that Hannah too would have remained barren like Michal, David's wife.

JESUS CHRIST
Jesus Christ will always represent for us be the personification of the servant's heart to us. He demonstrated the true servant's heart in all of its various aspects. Jesus Christ knew what awaited Him when He left Heaven to become the baby in the manger.
Jesus Christ grew up in a place where He would have seen crucifixions, and He would have realised the pain and suffering the condemned went through. Jesus knew what was in store for Him because he forewarned His disciples about His impending death. We never see Jesus complaining about the fact He had to suffer for the sins of humanity. Jesus is never depicted as showing any kind of insurrection to His Father in Heaven; rather, He was obedient to all the demands placed on Him in His capacity as Lamb of God.

In a moment of extreme torture, Jesus is shown in the Garden of Gethsemane praying, whilst His disciples snored. Even during this period, Jesus did not complain, but meekly accepted that the Father's will had to be accomplished no matter what. Looking at the life of Jesus, there are many sacrifices that He made whilst still on the earth, which perhaps we have not been called to, but that we should be aware of so that we can understand the depth of the requirements of the servant's heart.

Jesus never had a home, was rejected by His community, relinquished His rights to an earthly family, relinquished all His status as the Son of God, and accepted that the humans He was sent to redeem, would be the very ones who would torture Him. Jesus loved every one of the people around Him. He never ridiculed, harassed, discouraged or rejected any of the people He was sent to save.

Perhaps the most vivid example of Jesus exhibiting the servant's heart would be during His crucifixion, He asked the Father to forgive the people who were crucifying and mocking Him, because they did not understand what they were doing. You have to have a heart softer than jelly, to be able to feel that your shoulders are being dislocated, to feel yourself suffocating, to have nails in your hands and feet, no skin left on your back that is now being rubbed against a wooden cross, and to still have the capacity to forgive. We have a lot to learn.

DAVID

David's entire life revolved around his relationship with God. David's heart is seen in the Psalms that he penned, as well as in the records of his life in the Old Testament. David knew that his heart had to be soft before the Lord at all times. But, like us, even David sinned and allowed his heart to harden. This caused such a rift between David and God that David wrote Psalm 51 to express his repentance.

In the inident where his illegitimate child died because of the sin with Bathsheba, David fasted until the hour the child died, and immediately got up and went and worshipped the Lord in the Temple. David knew God is Sovereign, and gave God the honour and glory that God deserves, despite the pain he was in because of the circumstances he had created for himself.

EPAPHRAS

Epaphras was probably one of the founding members of the Colossian Church. He was a man whose life was considered an example of servant hood and faithful ministry.

Introducing Colossians

Background: Paul had never visited Colosse, a small town in the province of Asia, about one hundred miles east of Ephesus. The Colossian Church was an outgrowth of his three-year ministry in Ephesus about a.d. 52–55 (see Acts 19:10; 20:31). Epaphras, a native of the town, and probably a convert of the apostle, was likely the Church's founder and leader (1:7–8; 4:12–13).[99]

Dr. CLARE ERNSTZEN

Colossians 1:3-8,

³ We give thanks to the God and Father of our Lord Jesus Christ, praying always for you, ⁴ since we heard of your faith in Christ Jesus and of your love for all the saints; ⁵ because of the hope which is laid up for you in heaven, of which you heard before in the word of the truth of the gospel, ⁶ which has come to you, as *it has* also in all the world, and is bringing forth fruit, as *it is* also among you since the day you heard and knew the grace of God in truth; ⁷ as you also learned from Epaphras, our dear fellow servant, who is a faithful minister of Christ on your behalf, ⁸ who also declared to us your love in the Spirit.[100]

Colossians 4:12,

¹² Epaphras, who is *one* of you, a bondservant of Christ, greets you, always laboring fervently for you in prayers, that you may stand perfect and complete in all the will of God.[101]

Philemon 23-24

²³ Epaphras, my fellow prisoner in Christ Jesus, greets you, ²⁴ *as do* Mark, Aristarchus, Demas, Luke, my fellow laborers.[102] Epaphras, who is one of you, a servant of Christ Jesus, saluteth you,—for Epaphras see on 1:7 and Philemon 23. He was either a native or inhabitant of Colossae. Paul uses doulos, a bond servant (of Christ Jesus) only of himself, Timothy and Epaphras to describe individuals; elsewhere he uses it in the plural. It may be gathered therefore that Epaphras had rendered special service in connection with the gospel.[103]

When we live as sincere servants of the Lord and not of men, we find ourselves doing God's will, not by coercion, but from the heart: "Not with eye service, as men pleasers, but as bondservants of Christ, doing the will of God from the heart" (Eph 6.6)[104]

1 Peter 2:13-16,

¹³ Therefore submit yourselves to every ordinance of man for the Lord's sake, whether to the king as supreme, ¹⁴ or to governors, as to those who are sent by him for the punishment of evildoers and *for the* praise of those who do good. ¹⁵ For this is the will of God, that by doing good you may put to silence the ignorance of foolish men— ¹⁶ as free, yet not using liberty as a cloak for vice, but as bondservants of God.[105]

Free... but as bondservants (2:16): Peters's whole idea of submission may be summed up here. As individuals, we are free (*eleutheros,* Strong's #1658), "not under legal obligation, freeborn, able to move on our own and come and go as we please." But as Christians, we willfully exchange our independence for servanthood (*doulos,* "slavery" Strong's #1401) under God and the authorities He sets (2:14, 16). By doing so, we become "free to serve the Lord in all the ways that are consistent with His word, will, nature, and holiness." [106]

CHAPTER 7

CHARACTERS IN THE BIBLE THAT REFUSED THE CHANGE
OF HEART OFFERED TO THEM BY THE LORD.

SAUL
Saul is one of the sadder cases mentioned in the Bible. This man had everything going for him, and as is our wont as humans, threw everything away because of pride and arrogance. Saul was chosen by lot to be king, and shown acceptance by God; he was anointed by Samuel and made king over Israel. Even though Saul was handsome, he lacked the depth of character required for a king. As a result, he allowed pride in his position to cause rebellion to rise in his heart, and he did not learn to lean on God.

Saul needed the approval of man more than God, and made his fatal mistake by not waiting for Samuel to offer the sacrifices to God, but offered them himself. Saul suffered because of his inferiority complex, and tried to fulfil other positions in an effort to impress his soldiers.

When rebuked by Samuel for this breach of position, Saul hardened his heart, and did not see Samuel again. We see Saul eventually approaching a witch to tell him the future, showing exactly how far Saul had fallen from his relationship with God. Saul was wounded in battle and eventually took his own life.

AHAB AND JEZEBEL
Ahab and Jezebel could possibly be seen as the 'Bonny and Clyde' of the Bible. Ahab was a weak pawn, under the clutches of his wife Jezebel. Jezebel set up various shrines to different gods, and ordained priests for these shines. Jezebel is still seen today as a spiritual onslaught by people who hide behind the figurehead in authority, but are really running the entire show. Jezebel had no qualms about giving orders for Ahab to follow.

Ahab was shown the hand of God on various occasions by Elijah, during the drought, during the sacrifice on the mountain where God lit up the altar, when Elijah run past the chariot, and when the rain return after Elijah prayed. Not one of these miracles, however, changed Ahab's mind enough to stand up to Jezebel. Ahab preferred to remain under her dictatorship.

Jezebel too, remained unmoved by these same experiences, and was later eaten by the dogs outside the city gates.

HOPHNI AND PHINEAS
Hophni and Phineas were the two sons of Eli the High Priest. They had been reared in the Temple under Eli, but had turned away from God's laws and had become wicked. They were prostituting themselves with the women who came to the meetings at the Temple. When Eli confronted his sons about this sin, they ignored their father, and the Scriptures tell us that this was because God had already desired to kill them. We cannot continue in known sin and expect God to allow us to sin against Him without consequences. (1 Samuel 2:25)

HAMAN
Haman showed his rejection of the servant's heart by his continual efforts to be recognised and promoted by man. Even when Haman had to parade Mordecai through the streets, as praise for the foiled assassination attempt on the king, Haman did not register he was on a loosing spree. Haman had not learned that it is God who promotes and God who sets people in their places. He remained under the impression he was being short changed by the people in authority around him, and subsequently tried to impress everyone.

ANANIAS AND SAPPHIRA
Ananias and Sapphira are examples of people who pretended to have the servant's heart. They conformed outwardly to the practice of the New Church, but decided in their hearts they would not give all the earnings from the sale of their property, for fear of becoming destitute. They had not learned to trust God completely with their finances and situations, and like the Israelites of old, kept looking back at what they had had versus what they could see in their limited minds of their future.

The fact they decided to lie to the Apostles, and to the Holy Spirit shows that the hardness of their hearts had not been softened, that they had only decided to follow the flow rather than experience this change personally.

JUDAS ISCARIOT
Judas Iscariot walked for three years with Jesus literally, but still did not have the change of heart that could have saved him from destruction. Jesus knew He was to be betrayed but this did not prevent Him from loving and accepting Judas who determined to follow his own agenda and so showed his hardness of heart.

Many people think that if we could see the power of God moving through the earth today, then perhaps more people would turn and dedicate their lives to our Saviour. Judas remains historical proof that this does not work. Judas ate, slept, walked with and listened to Jesus for three years, but still had his hand in the treasury, and managed to avoid being touched by the Master. If we do not wish to submit to the leading of the Holy Spirit, He will never force Himself on us.

CHAPTER 8
WHAT ARE THE PRACTICAL COMPONENTS OF A SERVANT'S HEART?

To understand the practical components of a servant's heart, we firstly need to ask ourselves what worship is, and then, of course, deduce what worship is not.

There are various words in both the Old and New Testaments that have been translated as the English word 'worship'.

Old Testament words :-

Shachah   To bow down (Genesis 24:26, 48)

This means to prostrate oneself, to crouch, bow down, fall down, humbly beseech, to do obeisance. This word is demonstrated by Abraham's servant bowing to Rebekah, Joseph's sheaves bowing, Ruth bowing to Boaz, and David bowing before Saul. This honour was shown to equals, kings and deity. Therefore it could mean honouring God without the physical manifestation of prostration. The usual mode of this salutation involved the person falling on their knees and touching their forehead to the ground, revealing the vulnerable back of the neck in submission.

Abad   To serve, the labour of servants (Exodus 3:12)

This word means to serve, be made to serve, toil, be worked, work, to till, to plough, to make weary, fatigued, to work as a slave, enslave, to be honoured, to worship, cause to worship.

New Testament words :-

Latreuo   To serve (Philippians 3:3)

This word refers to a wholehearted sacrificial service to the Lord that is part of our true worship. This refers particularly to the performance of the Levitical service. This implies a hired servant versus the slave, a service that was not out of compulsion.

Proskuneo   To kiss the hand towards in reverence (Matthew 28:9)

This word refers to an act of homage and reverence. This was shown by the women at the empty tomb, when they fell at Jesus' feet, clasped them and worshipped God.

Sebomai   To venerate, devotion (Acts 18:7)

This word originally meant to fall back, before. This bodily manifestation was meant to exhibit an attitude of respect and awe.

As we can see, this word worship means different things on different occasions, depending on the situation and the heart attitude of the person, as well as the relationship experienced with God.

Author Robert G. Rayburn states,
The worship of God is at once the true believer's most important activity and at the same time it is one of the most tragically neglected activities in the average evangelical Church today .... There remains, however, among sincere believers ..... a woeful ignorance concerning the significance of true worship and the means of obtaining the blessing of *rich, rewarding corporate worship.*
(Robert G, Rayburn, O Come Let Us Worship. Corporate Worship in the Evangelical Church (Grand Rapids: Baker Book *House, 1980), p.11. Extracted from Exalt Him!, Terry Wardle)*

David Watson spoke particularly about the priority of worship within the Christian community. He said that worship:

- *Is the first and great commandment: we should love the Lord our God. (Mark 12:30)*
- *Is the first action we should take when we come into God's presence: we should "enter his gates with thanksgiving" (Psalm 100:4)*
- *Is the first response we should make when we come to Christ: "Offer spiritual sacrifices acceptable to God through Jesus Christ" (1 Peter 2:5)*
- *Is the first mark of the Holy Spirit in our lives: "God sent the Spirit of his Son into our hearts, the Spirit who calls out, 'Abba, Father' " (Galatians 4:6)*
- *Was the first sign of the Holy Spirit at Pentecost: "All of them were filled with the Holy Spirit and began to speak in other tongues" (Acts 2:4)*
- *Was the first priority of the early Church: "They continued meeting together in the temple courts.....praising God" (Acts 2:41-47)*
- *Was their first reaction when in trouble: "When they heard this, they raised their voices together in prayer to God" (Acts 4:24)*
- *Is the first essential when listening to God: "While*

> *they were worshipping and fasting, the Holy Spirit said...." (Acts 13:2)*
- *Is the ceaseless language of Heaven: "Day and night they never stop saying:'Holy, holy, holy' " (Revelation 4:8)*[107]

When considering how a person with a servant's heart would worship the Lord, various issues come into focus. Firstly, we will consider the private or closet time of worship. This is when the person spends time alone with the Lord in the sanctuary of his or her own quiet place. For different people this is definitely different areas, for example one person will pray in the sanctuary of the study and another in the quietness of an office before opening time, some will go to a secluded spot in the woods.

There will be times when music is used to enter the presence of the Lord, be this instrumental or music with lyrics. I find that sometimes the lyrics have a tendency to withdraw the brain from focusing on the Lord, and the words of the song become the focus. Whilst this is sometimes needed as the Holy Spirit reveals instances in our lives that He would deal with through the ministry of others, there are times when this can become a hindrance to the time of worship. Music without lyrics allows you to make up your own words as you spend time focusing on the Lord, His goodness, grace and glory. There are also times when even instrumental music can hinder the presence of the Lord, and we should never prescribe atmospheres and actions, (like dim lights, circular tables and holding hands... just kidding!), lest we too become caught up in rituals and lose the "ever changing" but "always the same" dynamic of the presence of the Living God.

The attitude of the heart during these times of worship varies, but perhaps the most important is the attitude of prostration as we wait before the Lord; aware of His awesome presence, and waiting for His commands. Sometimes there will be no commands, just the requirement that we prostrate ourselves before His Holiness. It is times like these when we catch glimpses of the glory we will see in Heaven. The stillness as our hearts are submitted to waiting, the gentleness as He washes over us, the tenderness as we feel His love, are all different aspects of this waiting period. This is not a time of uncomfortable silence where you are trying to blank out the thoughts bombarding your mind, nor a time of struggle to sit still long enough to warrant the "achievement" of being still in the Presence of the Lord. This is a time of Peace; time will suddenly have disappeared, the throne room and its occupants become the centre of your attention, the grace of God manifests itself as you 'stand' in the very centre of Holiness itself.

There are of course different types of prostration and like the Pharisee and the man in the Temple, the outward manifestation of lying face down in dusty carpets does not necessarily mean the heart is bowed before an Almighty God.

Dr. CLARE ERNSTZEN

Some of the people who stand expressionless, motionless and almost comatose are literally seated at the feet of the Father in their hearts in a way some more extroverted people will never understand. This however should not become an 'all stand still and not move' doctrine, but has to be led by the Holy Spirit – if He wills to make you undignified during your time of worship as with David, then allow Him the privilege of leading you to new heights in your relationship with the Lord.

Secondly we will consider times of corporate worship. This is when we are involved in a meeting of the Church or Cell group, and a time of worship is encouraged. Unfortunately these times, depending on the size of the meeting, can be swamped with tradition and religion that completely outcasts the very God that the people are trying to contact. Once the worship team has managed to wind everyone up with a few praise songs and managed to almost remove the burdens the unsuspecting and uneducated Christians carry with them, then it is time to quietly enter the Lord's presence. In theory this is great, but when you have people shuffling about, children running up and down, it becomes rather strained for newcomers to the time of worship to experience exactly what worship is all about. This is why it is so important for believers to have times of worship alone, times when they enter the presence of the Lord and experience His greatness.

I have yet to hear a preacher preach on how to enter into worship, most new Christians are given the ten steps to salvation, told to make disciples, get baptised and then bumble their way along until either in desperation they reach breaking point and the Lord intervenes, or they slowly become dead and religious, thinking that if they follow rituals and traditions then they are serving the Lord.

And yet, there are a few who manage to steer clear of the religion and tradition trap and as these people become more familiar with their relationship with the Lord, and entering into times of personal worship becomes easier, we find that people learn the ability to lose themselves in the Presence of the Lord even during a corporate time of worship. Inhibitions and feelings of inferiority wane as the person learns to give completely of themselves in these times, no matter what the distractions around them.

How can we remotely consider that thirty seconds of silence in an atmosphere tense with parents waiting for a child to wriggle or cough or scream during a silence in Church as an atmosphere of worship? True enough this is all some people experience in their relationship with the Lord because of the lack of teaching and knowledge with regard to the time of worship. Hosea quotes how God's people are destroyed through a lack of knowledge. (Hosea 4:6) The Church today tends to consider the time of worship as the time the slower songs are sung, and we take up the offering as an act of worship, for that matter, why not take up the offering with a loud, raucous hand clapping, joyful song, as we are supposed to give with a grateful heart, not in sorrow and mourning to our God. Hmmmm – We could get ex-communicated for this comment!

Thirdly, there is a lifestyle of worship. This puts the entire servant's heart into a nutshell. The lifestyle becomes one of an attitude of worship to the Lord where the mind, body and spirit are subjected to the Will of God. This becomes a voluntary kind of lifestyle. Everything done is considered in the light of the effect it would have on the Father and whether or not glory would be given to the Father by the action. The Holy Spirit is encouraged to walk daily with the person, spending time speaking to the new heart, teaching, guiding and encouraging.

The new lifestyle begins with a renewed understanding of grace, no matter what the failures are, the goalpost set ahead is that of complete submission to the Will of God. This understanding of grace reveals itself as the person sees himself not in his own eyes but through the eyes of the Lord.

The servant's heart begins to associate responses and reactions with the effect they have on their relationship and fellowship with the Father. Fellowship is damaged as the person sins and is restored during confession and communication between God and the person. The servant's heart evaluates emotions, mood swings, outbursts of anger, and learns to hand them over to the Lord, realising many of the responses are because the heart has not died to self and is still being changed.

The relationship with the Father is at once submissive as well as responsive. Whilst the heart is submissive to the Will of the Father, and desires to see the Father enjoy and receive all the Glory, the heart is not completely without the ability to function independently. God does not wish us to become robots programmed to His every whim – He has angels that already adore Him and completely do His Will, we are supposed to be different in that we have the choice of whether or not we will follow His Will. The Servant's Heart will want to follow the Fathers Will in every aspect of life.

This will become the new lifestyle of worship, as the heart prostrates itself before the throne of grace and waits on the Lord. The picture of Jesus washing the disciples feet, the abandonment of self image, the ability to lower oneself to the level of least in the Kingdom of God, the knowledge that you live and breathe and have your being only through the grace of God, and the adoration that flows from this knowledge epitomises the prostration of the life of the servant's heart at the feet of God.

This lifestyle of worship flows from the depths of the soul and overflows as Jesus quoted like streams of living water. The focus of the individual becomes entirely God centred, desiring only to please the Father and give Him glory. A return of the wonder we experienced as a child for new things returns as the expectancy of God and the fulfilment of His promises is restored in our lives. We begin to understand the awe of the angels as they cry, "Holy, holy, holy", as we experience for ourselves the absolute joy in serving the King of Kings.

Songs of joy break forth, as the barren areas are watered in our lives, (Isaiah 54), we find we grow spiritually as our tents are stretched, and our vision is renewed and restored.

Defining Worship
Worship is an event and a process.

In the worship event, we gather to honor and revere Christ through certain patterns and traditions. Robert Webber writes, "The focus of worship is not human experience, not a lecture, nor entertainment, but Jesus Christ—his life, death and resurrection." Bob Sorge complements that thought, stating, "The goal for our worship should be that we come to the point when we do not see anyone or anything around us, but we become totally taken up with God. This is the supreme goal of worship: to see only the Lord." That is the worship event.

Then, with the event, there is the worship process. Simply stated, this refers to our discipleship—the maturation sequence in which we move from self-centeredness to Christ-centeredness. LaMar Boschman writes, "We must develop a life of worship, living in His presence, not just visiting on weekends. The Lord is looking for worshipers, not just worship."

Having established our objective—to become worshipers—let's investigate scriptural commands on the theme, taking as our key Psalm 113:3, "From the rising of the sun to its going down, the Lord's name is to be praised." These words encapsulate worship, both as an event and a process.

> These words encapsulate worship, both as an event and a process.[108]

CHAPTER 9
SERVANT LEADERSHIP

The Church today is vitally in need of servant leaders who will train up new disciples in the Way of the Lord. This cannot be a two-week – three-part course, but if we look at the life of Jesus, it can almost be seen as a requirement of full time learning on behalf of the student – and no I am not advocating only those who go through Bible School are eligible to be servant leaders, but it does take time and learning to become a servant leader.

Mostly it will take time to unlearn all the leadership skills we are so proud of!

Everyone agrees that there is an acute shortage of trained leadership at all levels in the Church in Africa today, especially given the current phenomenal rate of growth of the Christian community on the continent. But what kind of leaders do we need? What kinds of leaders should we be training to meet the future needs of our Churches in Africa?

Left to itself with these questions, the Church all too readily begins to copy the world's models of leadership. Seeing the styles of leadership in the world and he ways in which leaders are chosen there, Church members begin to copy these patterns within the Church. The world enters and begins to press the Church into its own mould.

When one enquires concerning the kind of leaders needed, the models that come to attention are, for example, that of the successful marketing executive, skilled in management, in getting programmes implemented and goals accomplished, or that the 'omni-competent' pastor whom the congregation must sheepishly look up to and obey! But the model of leadership that the Scriptures consistently commend to the people of God is instead what we may call the "Servant-Leader".

We find this model applied to all legitimate leadership in the Bible. In both the Old and New Testaments those who are qualified for appointment as leaders among the people of God are always appointed to *serve*. Whether appointed as prophets, priests or kings, they are not to lord it over God's people but to serve them.[109]

We need to be acutely aware that as a man has a tendency to take matters into his own hands when there is no apparent authority; and when ths happens – Chaos rules.

Judges 17:6,

⁶ In those days *there was* no king in Israel; everyone did *what was* right in his own eyes.[110]

In these Last Days, the Church cannot allow herself the apathy and self-destructive reasoning that has occurred in her for the past decades. She MUST arise and train her leaders in servant hood so that she may stand as the Bride of Christ; in her full arraignment – with every member God ordained for her; not missing some vital article of clothing – or person - because she was too apathetic to put it on – or train someone up! Every day that goes by in apathy, diminishes the beauty of the Bride of Christ for every soul that is lost detracts from her final beauty.

What are a few definitions of 'leadership' or 'leaders'?

Matthew 20:26-28,

²⁶ Yet it shall not be so among you; but whoever desires to become great among you, let him be your servant. ²⁷ And whoever desires to be first among you, let him be your slave— ²⁸ just as the Son of Man did not come to be served, but to serve, and to give His life a ransom for many."[111]

and,

A leader is one who commands. He occupies the chief position whether it is in the home or country, and by the very virtue of his position he has the resaponsibility to love and care for thos whom he leads. He is expected to have the final say in any decision or matter and, generally speaking, his word is law.

Also, he is responsible for the spiritual atmosphere of the home, Church or fellowship God has given to him. May it be one of love, joy, and peace. If he exudes that to his staff, they in turn will spread that throughout the Church and fellowship. The result will be that it will create an atmosphere of which others will say, "God is There – Jehovah Shammah."[112]

and,

Hebrews 5:1-4,

For every high priest taken from among men is appointed for men in things *pertaining* to God, that he may offer both gifts and sacrifices for sins. ² He can have compassion on those who are ignorant and going astray, since he himself is also subject to weakness. ³ Because of this he is required as for the people, so also for himself, to offer *sacrifices* for sins. ⁴ And no man takes this honor to himself, but he who is called by God, just as Aaron was.[113]

Success is within the reach of just about everyone. But ... personal success without leadership ability brings only limited effectiveness. A person's impact is only a fraction of what it could be with good leadership. The higher you want to climb, the more you need leadership. The greater the impact you want to make, the greater your influence needs to be.

Leadership ability is the lid that determines a person's level of effectiveness. The lower an individual's ability to lead, the lower the lid on his potential. The higher the leadership, the greater the effectiveness ... Your leadership ability – for better or for worse – always determines your effectiveness and the potential impact of your organization ... To reach the highest level of effectiveness, you have to raise the lid on your leadership ability.[114]

and,

Ask ten people to define leadership and you'll probably receive ten different answers. After more than four decades of observing leadership within my family and many years of developing my own leadership potential, I have come to this conclusion: *Leadership is influence.* That's it. nothing more; nothing less.[115]

and,

A sense of identity, a security that comes from knowing who one is, lies at the heart of leadership. Leadership is first of all not something one does but something one is. This comes out clearly in the story of Jesus when his Father affirms Him as His special son (Matt 3:17; Mark 1:11; Luke 3:22). Jesus operated out of a sense of quiet confidence that came from knowing who He was in his everlasting relationship with His Father.[116]

and,

The Bible *does* teach a double standard. there is a very high standard for Christians in general. There is an even higher standard for Christian leaders.

Martin Luther once said, "It is no small thing to stand before men in the place of God." That is what it means to be a Christian leader. Is that not what James meant when he wrote, "Let not many of you become teachers, my brethren, knowing that as such we shall incur a stricter judgment" (James 3:1)?

To my readers who are already Christian leaders or who aspire to Christian leadership, God requires more of you and me than He does of those he calls us to lead. We must count the cost. We must not aspire to Christian leadership unless we are willing to die to self, to fleshly lusts, to the pride of life (1 John 2:15–17).[117]

and,

"In short, the fundamental problem is the Corinthians' image of Christian leadership. At least some of them had created in their minds an image, largely shaped by the values of the culture, of a leader who had honor, power, spiritual gifts, rhetorical skills, good references and who would accept patronage. They looked, that is, for a Sophist, or at least a rhetorically adept philosophical teacher."[118]

and,

Lessons for Leaders (Mic. 3:11). Spiritual leadership is a sacred trust. Though often coveted by the spiritual neophyte, it is a costly role for anyone who serves in it. Leaders, believe that God will stop speaking in revelation to leaders who become mercenary in their ministries. Leaders, be warned: never, never set a price on your ministry. Never deceitfully seduce people to become your financial support by using psychological or spiritual manipulation.[119]

and,

'to relieve leadership, you make committees and boards; but to reproduce leadership, you make disciples' – Anne Ortlund [120]

and,

'It is no use walking anywhere to reach unless our walking is our preaching.' St Francis of Assisi [121]

and,

Leadership is not a responsibility afforded to only a few but a privilege given by God to all. For leading is simply guiding or influencing the way of another. And Jesus asked every believer to participate in showing others the way to eternal life (Acts 1:8).

So whether it is across the sea or across the street, as a state senator or a team mum, as a corporate executive or a PTA committee member, we have all been given the opportunity to lead and influence others, and to help them find their way to The Way, Jesus Christ. [122]

So now that we have covered some aspects of leadership, how do we use this to allow the Holy Spirit to change the heart of others?

Initially some of the questions that arise would include the following:

- How can you have a Servant's Heart and not loose your authority with your staff?
- If you are so busy running around serving everyone, how are you going to make sure the work get's done?

- Who is going to make decisions if everyone is submitting to the other?
- How can a management flow chart work in this kind of atmosphere?
- How do you implement this kind of management system if everyone on the staff has not been through the experience?
- What about people who do not appreciate this kind of management system and try to take advantage of the situation?
- Is there a 10 Commandment list for the workplace?
- Is it possible to have experienced a Servant's Heart and compartmentalise this experience so that it does not affect your office ethics?

Early on in a working career, most people will receive a set of guidelines regarding a system called performance review. These can either be encouraging or downright debilitating. These reviews can open the doors for all sorts of politically based agendas.

The ideal behind these assessments is that a manager would assess the strengths and weaknesses of a staff member and then evaluate them fairly on the execution of the tasks set in their job descriptions. The idea being that this should show the employee where they are falling short and encourage and reward those areas that he is excelling in or has shown improvement in.

The shepherds of Israel underwent a performance appraisal themselves, and this was their report back:

Ezekiel 34:1-10,
And the word of the Lord came to me, saying, [2] "Son of man, prophesy against the shepherds of Israel, prophesy and say to them, 'Thus says the Lord God to the shepherds: "Woe to the shepherds of Israel who feed themselves! Should not the shepherds feed the flocks? [3] You eat the fat and clothe yourselves with the wool; you slaughter the fatlings, *but* you do not feed the flock. [4] The weak you have not strengthened, nor have you healed those who were sick, nor bound up the broken, nor brought back what was driven away, nor sought what was lost; but with force and cruelty you have ruled them. [5] So they were scattered because *there was* no shepherd; and they became food for all the beasts of the field when they were scattered. [6] My sheep wandered through all the mountains, and

on every high hill; yes, My flock was scattered over the whole face of the earth, and no one was seeking or searching *for them.*" [7] 'Therefore, you shepherds, hear the word of the Lord: [8] "*As* I live," says the Lord God, "surely because My flock became a prey, and My flock became food for every beast of the field, because *there was* no shepherd, nor did My shepherds search for My flock, but the shepherds fed themselves and did not feed My flock"— [9] therefore, O shepherds, hear the word of the Lord! [10] Thus says the Lord God: "Behold, I *am* against the shepherds, and I will require My flock at their hand; I will cause them to cease feeding the sheep, and the shepherds shall feed themselves no more; for I will deliver My flock from their mouths, that they may no longer be food for them."[123]

We see from this passage the following:

1. The shepherds were supposed to feed the flock.
2. They were supposed to share the good food with the sheep, allowing the flock to become as fat and healthy as they were.
3. they were supposed to look after the sick and lame and find the lost.
4. The sheep were in danger from wild animals because of a lack of care.
5. The shepherds were to be held accountable for the loss of sheep.
6. God would remove their position of caregiver to His flock.

Now, the above can be instrumental in your care of the people given to you to look after. As a Christian, you are required by God to be accountable for the flock He has given you. There can be no half measures here, God is not going to give you a flock and allow you to selectively look after the sheep you choose; He requires all are looked after with the same amount of commitment. Also, God is not necessarily referring to a Church flock, but to any group of people you have been placed in leadership over.

So, where do you start looking after your flock with a Servant's Heart? Jesus reiterated the shepherds' role in the following passage.

John 10:11-16,

[11] "I am the good shepherd. The good shepherd gives His life for the sheep. [12]

The Servant's Heart

But a hireling, *he who is* not the shepherd, one who does not own the sheep, sees the wolf coming and leaves the sheep and flees; and the wolf catches the sheep and scatters them. [13] The hireling flees because he is a hireling and does not care about the sheep. [14] I am the good shepherd; and I know My *sheep,* and am known by My own. [15] As the Father knows Me, even so I know the Father; and I lay down My life for the sheep. [16] And other sheep I have which are not of this fold; them also I must bring, and they will hear My voice; and there will be one flock *and* one shepherd.[124]

I would consider the primary area to be food for the flock. If you, as a leader, have had spiritual nourishment, and this has made you healthy and well fed, you are accountable to make sure the flock you have also feeds from the same revelation you have.

No, we are not talking about three hour preaching sessions in staff meetings twice a week. You have to lead by example. If you are teaching your staff caring for an individual matters, you are going to have to be the one who delivers the chicken soup, or the one who collects their children from school when a parent is ill. We are talking about practically showing your heart.

John 21:15-19,
[15] So when they had eaten breakfast, Jesus said to Simon Peter, "Simon, *son* of Jonah, do you love Me more than these?"
>He said to Him, "Yes, Lord; You know that I love You."
>He said to him, "Feed My lambs."
>
>>[16] He said to him again a second time, "Simon, *son* of Jonah, do you love Me?"
>
>He said to Him, "Yes, Lord; You know that I love You."
>He said to him, "Tend My sheep."
>
>>[17] He said to him the third time, "Simon, *son* of Jonah, do you love Me?" Peter was grieved because He said to him the third time, "Do you love Me?" And he said to Him, "Lord, You know all things; You know that I love You."
>
>Jesus said to him, "Feed My sheep. [18] Most assuredly, I say to you, when you were younger, you girded yourself and walked where you wished; but when you are old, you will stretch out your hands, and another
>
>will gird you and carry *you* where you do not wish." [19] This He spoke, signifying by what death he would glorify God. And when He had spoken this, He said to him, "Follow Me."[125]

1 Peter 5:2-5,

[2] Shepherd the flock of God which is among you, serving as overseers, not by

compulsion but willingly, not for dishonest gain but eagerly; ³ nor as being lords over those entrusted to you, but being examples to the flock; ⁴ and when the Chief Shepherd appears, you will receive the crown of glory that does not fade away. ⁵ Likewise you younger people, submit yourselves to *your* elders. Yes, all of *you* be submissive to one another, and be clothed with humility, for

> "God resists the proud,
> But gives grace to the humble."[126]

1 Thessalonians 5:12-15,

¹² And we urge you, brethren, to recognize those who labor among you, and are over you in the Lord and admonish you, ¹³ and to esteem them very highly in love for their work's sake. Be at peace among yourselves.

> ¹⁴ Now we exhort you, brethren, warn those who are unruly, comfort the fainthearted, uphold the weak, be patient with all. ¹⁵ See that no one renders evil for evil to anyone, but always pursue what is good both for yourselves and for all.[127]

Matthew 7:12,

¹² Therefore, whatever you want men to do to you, do also to them, for this is the Law and the Prophets.[128]

Lessons for Leaders (Zeph. 3:2-4)

The wise leader accepts the Scripture's testimony and rejects the prevailing humanistic doctrine that teaches man's intrinsic goodness. An unteachable attitude is the tip of the iceberg of ungodliness. This wisdom should influence one's self-view, causing all of us to guard ourselves from insincerity and pride in any of its manifestations.

Leaders, understand that the clearest evidence that someone does not trust the Lord or seek Him diligently is a rebellious, disobedient, and unteachable nature.

Leaders, avoid being among those who speak loudly, who promise great things, but produce nothing that lasts or bears fruit in the long run.

Leaders, avoid diligently any form of arrogance or pride in your ministry. Do not profane the ministry by mishandling God's Word in any way. Never teach your own opinion of God's Word. [129]Why did the Lord urge the faithful remnant to wait for the day of the Lord? (Zeph. 3:8; see 1:2, 3 and Hab. 2:3) [130]

In light of Jesus' own example—particularly in giving up His own life as a "ransom for many" (Matt. 20:28)—we can observe that servant-leadership means:
- seeing ourselves as called by God to serve/lead others;
- knowing intimately the people we serve/lead;
- caring deeply about the people we serve/lead; and
- being willing to sacrifice our own convenience to meet the needs of the

people we serve/lead. [131]

When choosing a particular check list for today's servant-leader, there are various areas to keep in mind. Above all, remember no check list will ever bring you closer to God these are just guidelines to keep you on track. Check lists will more than likely put you back under law than set you free under grace, so be very careful how you begin to implement anything in your life. Make certain the Holy Spirit is the One leading you in change and not your own good intentions.

There are a vast number of books on the subject of leadership, leadership skills, management tools, etc. all written by people who have researched these areas with great dexterity. As this book is not a book on leadership training, but rather a guideline to a particular area of spiritual growth, we will not go into the ten steps of leadership.

Here are some tips for those who desire to lead God's way.

- Develop an intimate relationship and walk with God.
- Live a life focused on doing the thing God has called you to do, and do it God's way. Be led by the Holy Spirit. Let Him set the agenda. Live a disciplined life so as to yield maximum fruitage.
- Pray about the type of ministry God would have you develop. Will it be a leader-centered or every-believer-a-priest ministry? In either case, seek to enable each believer you lead to reach his or her full potential of growth and ministry in Christ.
- Be an emissary of love to a world that is hurting.
- Let it be known that your sufficiency is not of yourself but of God. The miracles you have experienced and the achievement of things thought impossible all point to the One who gave the grace and who released His power to bring it all about.
- Be one through whom the Spirit of God can speak a fresh word to the Church. Preach and teach the Word with the anointing of the Spirit and be a vessel ready to speak the extemporaneous word of prophecy when it is the will of the Spirit to do so.
- Be rich in the knowledge of the Bible. [132]

The following are a few pertinent areas, but are by no means exhaustive:

Accountability

You need to be accountable to someone - specifically someone human. There must be a structure that you report within; someone who you can turn to in times of distress, in times of query. Someone who will tell you the truth and will support you through your good times and especially your bad times. Someone who will tell you the truth when your preaching is dry, and will be with you when you need restoration.

Be yourself

Why make the Holy Spirit work through your 'personality disorder' before He can work in the people around you?

Commitment

Your commitment to God, your family, your job, and your beliefs will all be tested. Make certain at all times that you are not overcommitted, that you are committed to the correct things that God desires you be committed to.

2 Corinthians 4:8-10,

8 *We are* hard-pressed on every side, yet not crushed; *we are* perplexed, but not in despair; **9** persecuted, but not forsaken; struck down, but not destroyed— **10** always carrying about in the body the dying of the Lord Jesus, that the life of Jesus also may be manifested in our body.[133]

A leading national secular publication did an article on the rise of megachurches in America. the writer of the article talked about the fact that many of the new Chruches had done away with crosses, robes, spires, pipe organs, old hymns, hard pews, kneeling and collection plates. Instead these super-churches of the future offer multimedia worship and view their congregation as customers. Many of the leaders of these new churches are attempting to reach a new generation, which they believe does not relate to the cultural settings of the past.

Whatever shape and form the church of the future takes, the key to its vitality and authenticity lies in how closely it adheres to the Biblical model. Fortunately, God has given Christian leaders a handbook and blue print for building the Church—the Bible. In addition, the apostle Paul has timely instructions for those who lead God's people in today's society.

Customs and culture often change. There is nothing inherently spiritual about such things as pews, spires, and pipe organs. The first-century Church simply met in people's houses. Although cultural aspects of the Christian faith can and do provide a rich source of inspiration to many people, some people can be reached only by different forms of religious style. In a culture which emphasizes the now and the immediate, we do not want to make the mistake of cutting ourselves off from our spiritual heritage and history. Many of the great hymns and traditional ways of doing things can provide for an abundance of powerful spiritual nourishment. At the same time we want to be open to new forms of worship the Holy Spirit inspires today.

The key to staying on course and building Churches and ministries as God would have us build them is to be people who intimately know the Word of God and who pray and seek God's face with all our heart, soul, and mind. If we stay immersed in God's Word and follow hard after Jesus Christ, then whatever outward form the Church takes will be guided by Him. After all, it is His Church we are building. [134]

Delegation
When you find yourself in a position of leadership, the only way to train up new leaders is a really drastic step called delegation. This spells the following:
- It will mean that you will have to ask others for help = vulnerability,
- It will mean that you will be let down = vulnerability,
- It will mean additional frustration as you need more help = vulnerability,
- You will wonder why you are in this position = vulnerability

You get the picture...

Empathy
Empathy understands what other people are going through, mainly because you have had similar experiences.
Empathy is the capacity for sharing vicariously the feelings and emotions of others. Our tendency is to be jealous when others rejoice, and to pass by when they mourn. God's way is to enter into the joys and sorrows of those around us. [135]

Romans 12:15,

[15] Rejoice with those who rejoice, and weep with those who weep.[136]

Proverbs 14:10,
> [10] The heart knows its own bitterness,
> And a stranger does not share its joy.[137]
>
> One of the most significant proverbs on the feelings and responses of an individual is this: no one really knows another's sorrows or joys. Empathy is an approximate art, never an exact science. Yet one is reminded of the words of the wonderful spiritual, "Nobody knows ... but Jesus!"[138]
>
> **COMFORT**. (Ps. 23:4) *nacham* (nah-chahm); Strong's #5162: To comfort, console, extend compassion, sigh with one who is grieving; to

repent. Nacham originally may have meant "to breathe intensely because of deep emotion." In some references, the word is translated "repent," the idea being that regret causes deep sighing. In its sense of comfort, nacham does not describe casual sympathy, but rather deep empathy. It is like "weeping with those who weep," or actually "sighing with those who sigh." From nacham are derived the names "Nahum" ("Comforting") and Nehemiah ("Comfort of Yahweh").

Also (Acts 9:31) paraklesis (par-ak-lay-sis); Strong's #3874: A calling alongside to help, to comfort, to give consolation or encouragement. The paraklete is a strengthening presence, one who upholds those appealing for assistance. Paraklesis (comfort) can come to us both by the Holy Spirit (v. 31) and by the Scriptures (Rom. 15:4).[139]

Job's friends could have learned about empathy before they spent their breath criticizing his life. Even when they had spent seven days and nights sitting with him in his grief they did not fully understand or appreciate his needs.

Job 2:11-13

[11] Now when Job's three friends heard of all this adversity that had come upon him, each one came from his own place—Eliphaz the Temanite, Bildad the Shuhite, and Zophar the Naamathite. For they had made an appointment together to come and mourn with him, and to comfort him. [12] And when they raised their eyes from afar, and did not recognize him, they lifted their voices and wept; and each one tore his robe and sprinkled dust on his head toward heaven. [13] So they sat down with him on the ground seven days and seven nights, and no one spoke a word to him, for they saw that *his* grief was very great.[140]

So they sat down with him upon the ground seven days and seven nights and none spake a word unto him: for they saw that his grief was very great. Seven days and nights was the traditional period of mourning for the dead (Gen 50:10; I Sam 31:13). Although a few assume that the mourning was for the death of Job's children, most take it to be related to Job himself and his degraded situation, humanly speaking. Not everyone agrees as to why the friends remained silent for seven days. Some cite the Hebrew tradition that the person in mourning must speak to the visitor first. In that case, it would have been impolite for the three friends to break the silence. Others see in the silence a confusion on the part of the friends concerning what to say. For additional possibilities with regard to this silence see Albert Barnes, The Book of Job, pp. 36–37.

Job needed understanding, empathy, and confidence to be shown in him. Instead, he got judgment, condemnation, and sermons. A careful study of the following discourses should be required study for those who plan to counsel people. George Adam Smith writes, "The author shows how all three comforters of Job misunderstood the heart; how little they have fathomed human experience; how easily worn out their love and patience; how they prefer to vindicate their own views of God to saving the soul of their brother; and how above all they commit the sin of not perceiving that God Himself may be working directly in that brother's heart, and purposes to teach them more than they can ever teach him. Love was what he looked for, and trust: but they gave him argument which for a time only drove him further from God" (Modern Criticism and the Old Testament, pp. 298–299).

There is one redeeming factor in the actions of the friends. What they had to say about Job they said to his face, and not to others behind his back.[141]

A Kinder, Gentler Counselor

Elihu sat on the sidelines while Eliphaz, Bildad, and Zophar exhausted their pleas to Job (Job 32:4–5). Apparently Elihu assumed that these three counselors would be more knowledgeable than he because of their age. Yet when it became evident that they lacked convincing arguments, he offered a new perspective through four back-to-back addresses (Job 32:5–33:33; 34:1–37; 35:1–16; 36:1–37:24).

Elihu turned out to be far more empathetic in his treatment of Job. For example, he allowed for the possibility that neither Job's circumstances nor his rebuttals to his three friends' remarks necessarily implied sin or guilt. Instead, he suggested—probably correctly—that Job was being disciplined and refined by fire for his greater good, or to teach greater truth.

Perhaps because of the merit of Elihu's arguments, God did not reproach him the way he did Job's three other friends (Job 42:7–9). Apparently God did not take issue with what the young counselor had said. But Elihu's explanation for Job's condition did not go far enough.

There is no higher principle of justice than God's to which humanity can appeal. God Himself is the ultimate standard of justice. We need appeal to God alone for mercy or vindication. We may also appeal for greater ability to understand our experience, but we have no guarantee of receiving that—at least not on this side of heaven.

Elihu and counselors like him are to be commended for first trying to put themselves in another person's place. By observing and listening before speaking, they are better equipped to apply abstract theological concepts to real, live human beings in sensitive, compassionate ways.[142]

Here are a few practical illustrations of empathy at work.
The popular writer F. W. Boreham once lost patience with a difficult man named Crittingden, who said and wrote many critical words. Boreham, angered beyond endurance, finally wrote a flaming letter designed to sting and rebuke

the complainer. He walked to the mailbox to post the letter. It was a lovely night for a walk, and he passed by the mailbox without dropping the letter in. He said to himself, "I'll mail it on the way back."

A quarter of a mile further on, he met a friend who said, "Poor old Crittingden is dead."

Boreham was shocked. "Is he, indeed? When did this happen?"

"Oh, he died suddenly—early this afternoon. It's really for the best, you know. He's had a hard time. You know all about it, I suppose?"

"No, I don't."

"Oh, I thought everybody knew. He only had two children, a son and a daughter. The son was killed soon after his wife died, and the daughter lost her mind and is in the asylum. Poor old Crittingden never got over it. It soured him."

Boreham returned to his fireside that night, humbled and ashamed. He tore the letter into small fragments and burned them one by one. And as he knelt before the blaze, he prayed that he, in days to come, might find the grace to deal gently and lovingly with difficult people, even as he wished they might have the grace to treat him. [143]

In 1873, a Belgian Catholic priest named Joseph Damien De Veuster was sent to minister to lepers on the Hawaiian Island of Molokai. When he arrived, he immediately began to meet each one of the lepers in the colony in hopes of building a friendship. But wherever he turned, people shunned him. It seemed as though every door was closed. He poured his life into his work, erecting a chapel, beginning worship services and pouring out his heart to the lepers. But it was to no avail. No one responded to his ministry. After twelve years Father Damien decided to leave.

Dejectedly, he made his way to the docks to board a ship to take him back to Belgium. As he stood on the dock, he wrung his hands nervously, recounting his futile ministry among the lepers. As he did he looked down at his hands, he noticed some mysterious white spots and felt some numbness. Almost immediately he knew what was happening to his body. He had contracted leprosy.

It was then that he knew what he had to do. He returned to the leper colony and to his work. Quickly the word about his disease spread through the colony. Within a matter of hours everyone knew. Hundreds of them gathered outside his hut, they understood his pain, fear, and uncertainty about the future.

But the biggest surprise was the following Sunday. As Father Damien arrived at the Chapel, he found hundreds of worshipers there. By the time the service began, there were many more with standing room only, and many gathered outside the chapel. His ministry became enormously successful. The reason? He was one of them. He understood and empathized with them.[144]

Stephen Covey writes in his Seven Habits of Highly Effective People about an experience he had on a subway in New York. It was Sunday morning, and the passengers were sitting quietly, napping, reading the paper, lost in thought. But the peaceful scene changed when a man and his children suddenly boarded. The children were loud and rambunctious, and they disrupted the entire car.

The man sat down beside Covey, seemingly oblivious to the situation. The children were yelling, throwing things, and even grabbing people's papers. It was very disturbing, and yet the man did nothing.

Covey fought the feelings of irritation that rose in him, but as the confusion grew worse he finally turned and said, "Sir, your children are really disturbing a lot of people. I wonder if you couldn't control them a little more?"

The man lifted his gaze as if coming to himself, then he said softly, "Oh, you're right. I guess I should do something about it. We just came from the hospital where their mother died about an hour ago. I don't know what to think, and I guess they don't know how to handle it either."Covey later wrote, Can you imagine what I felt at that moment? My paradigm shifted. Suddenly I saw things differently, and because I saw differently, I thought differently, I felt differently, I behaved differently. My irritation vanished … my heart was filled with the man's pain. Feelings of sympathy and compassion flowed freely. "Your wife just died? Oh, I'm so sorry! Can you tell me about it? What can I do to help?" Everything changed in an instant.[145]

In the comic strip Peanuts, Linus was watching a football game on television, cheering "Go! Go! Go!" When the game ended victoriously, he jumped up in a surge of emotion and ran out to find Charlie Brown.

"What a comeback!" he exclaimed. "The home team was behind six to nothing with only three seconds to play. They had the ball on their own one-yard line. The quarterback took the ball, faded back behind his own goal and threw a perfect pass to the left end who whirled away from four guys and ran in for the touchdown! The fans went wild! You should have seen them! And when they kicked the extra point, thousands of people ran onto the field laughing and screaming and rolling on the ground and hugging each other and everything!"Charlie Brown turned to him and asked, "How did the other team feel?"[146]

Financial Integrity
Never allow yourself to be put into a position where your financial integrity is in question, whether in your business or in your Church. Seek the appropriate financial wisdom from people who are gifted in this area – you would not ask a mechanic to fix a broken geyser – well you shouldn't, so don't ask a bankrupt gambling addicted salesman how to run your finances.

Exodus 18:21,
²¹ Moreover you shall select from all the people able men, such as fear God, men of truth, hating covetousness; and place *such* over them *to be*rulers of thousands, rulers of hundreds, rulers of fifties, and rulers of tens.[147]

Integrity

Ten Tests of Integrity
Psalm 15 lists ten marks of integrity. How does your life compare?
The person of integrity...
- walks uprightly. What is your basic ethical commitment? Are you out to honor the Lord or to serve yourself?
- works righteousness. What is the end result of your work? Are you promoting good in the world—or evil?
- speaks the truth. Are you in the habit of telling "little white lies" when it is necessary or convenient?
- does not backbite. Do you tear down others behind their back?
- does no evil to a neighbor. What is your policy on office politics? Do you believe in "doing unto others before they do unto you"?
- does not take up a reproach against a friend. How loyal are you? When everyone is down on a colleague, do you jump on the bandwagon, or do you offer support and seek fair play?
- honors those who fear the Lord, not the ungodly. What is the character of your best friends? What is their attitude toward God and the things of the Lord?
- keeps his word, even when it is costly. Are you trustworthy and reliable? Is your word your bond, or is there always a question whether you will follow through?
- does not practice usury. Do you make it harder or easier for poor people to gain the resources necessary to support themselves?
- does not take bribes. What would it take to get you to compromise your integrity?

Ethics and Character in Psalms
Over and over the Book of Psalms reminds us that what ultimately matters to God is the quality of our character (Ps. 37:27–29). The following psalms merit careful study if we want to pursue ethical decision-making and godly behavior:
- Psalm 26: Integrity is a reasonable basis for seeking the Lord's protection.
- Psalm 101: This psalm expresses some of the high ideals that the person of character will pursue.
- Psalm 119: God's Word provides clear guidelines for living with integrity.
- Psalm 141: This psalm is a prayer for help to maintain integrity when one is tempted to compromise.

Out of Sight, Out of Mind
In a sense, the chief butler owed his life to Joseph, who had correctly interpreted his dream (Gen. 40:9–13). All that Joseph asked in return was to be remembered once the butler was reinstalled in his position. The account implies that the butler agreed to do so. But like so many people, he forgot his promise once he was out of trouble (Gen. 40:23). It was not until two full years had gone by (Gen. 41:1) and Pharaoh happened to have a dream of his own that the butler remembered

his commitment, apparently with some guilt (Gen. 41:9).

The incident stands as a reminder to us all: When was the last time we agreed to do something? Have we followed through on our commitment? Or have we slipped into the common pattern of "out of sight, out of mind"? God wants us to be people of our word (Matt. 5:37).

Risk and Responsibility
An inheritance can be a blessing to a family, but it can also be a terrible curse that divides family members. A lot depends on who manages the disbursements of the assets and how well they do their job.

When Israel divided Canaan, it was Joshua's job to act somewhat like a trustee of an estate, making sure that each tribe received the lands to which it was entitled. It was a delicate job that required him to act with great integrity. Otherwise he might be charged with being unfair in assigning boundaries or with neglecting commitments previously made by Moses.

Joshua handled his responsibility by seeking the welfare of the twelve tribes first before asking for land himself (Josh. 19:49–50). In doing so, he ran the risk of having to settle for a leftover, second-best portion of Canaan. But he avoided any question of impropriety.

This policy was in marked contrast to that of the Canaanite and Amorite kings of the city-states that the Israelites were inheriting. The pagan kings generally lorded it over their people, choosing for themselves the first and the best. Joshua took the posture of a "servant-leader," forsaking greed and self-interest in order to seek the highest good for his people (see Matt. 20:25–28).

Joshua's example is worth emulating today. As we accept responsibilities and make decisions that affect others, our challenge is to do the right thing by seeking justice, trusting God to work out the details of our own welfare.
For more on this topic, see HONESTY, "Free to Be Honest," page 202.[148]

INTEGRITY — honesty, sincerity, singleness of purpose. In the Old Testament, Noah (Gen. 6:9), Abraham (Gen. 17:1), Jacob (Gen. 25:27), David (1 Kin. 9:4), and Job (Job 1:1, 8; 2:3, 9; 4:6; 27:5; 31:6) were called people of integrity. Although Jesus did not use the word "integrity," he called for purity of heart (Matt. 5:8), singleness of purpose (Matt. 6:22), and purity of motive (Matt. 6:1–6).[149]

Goals
Goals are a seriously dynamic structure; dynamic in they must be ever-changing – the flexibility to allow you growth to move with the times but also rigid enough to stop you from going off on a tangent that would decimate the end result of

the goal.

Proverbs 4:25-27,
> ²⁵ Let your eyes look straight ahead,
> And your eyelids look right before you.
> ²⁶ Ponder the path of your feet,
> And let all your ways be established.
> ²⁷ Do not turn to the right or the left;
> Remove your foot from evil.[150]

Motivation

We can never allow our motivation to waver. We need to be seriously grounded throughour our lives in the ministry so that we do not waver.

2 Corinthians 4:16-18,

¹⁶ Therefore we do not lose heart. Even though our outward man is perishing, yet the inward *man* is being renewed day by day. ¹⁷ For our light affliction, which is but for a moment, is working for us a far more exceeding *and* eternal weight of glory, ¹⁸ while we do not look at the things which are seen, but at the things which are not seen. For the things which are seen *are* temporary, but the things which are not seen *are* eternal.[151]

We do not respond to God's call because of any guarantees of a secure position. It is not about us. It is about God's glory and the sheep He wants us to care for and equip.
I have heard of people saying, "I will plant a Church if you give me fifty people." Or, "I will plant a Church if you guarantee me a salary for six months or a year or two years." That is not the heart that God is looking for. The attitude He is looking for is one that is willing to go and do His will no matter what it costs. He is looking for people who are not so concerned with what they will get out of it, but who will respond because He has called them, even if they have to die in the process.[152]

Psalm 26:2,
> ² Examine me, O Lord, and prove me;
> Try my mind and my heart.[153]

Prophecies
when you are given prophecies to give to people, or when you receive them from someone else, be careful to test them as we are instructed to do in the Word.

1 Thessalonians 5:21,
> ²¹ Test all things; hold fast what is good.[154]

Jeremiah 30:2,
> ² "Thus speaks the Lord God of Israel, saying: 'Write in a book for yourself all the words that I have spoken to you.[155]

Habakkuk 2:2-4,
> ² Then the Lord answered me and said:
>
> "Write the vision
> And make *it* plain on tablets,
> That he may run who reads it.
>
> ³ For the vision *is* yet for an appointed time;
> But at the end it will speak, and it will not lie.
> Though it tarries, wait for it;
> Because it will surely come,
> It will not tarry.
>
> ⁴ "Behold the proud,
> His soul is not upright in him;
> But the just shall live by his faith.[156]

Erroneous prophecy did occur in the early Church; Paul had to address a case in Corinth (1 Cor. 12:1-3), and he tells the Corinthians to judge the prophecies (1 Cor. 14:29). Likewise, we need to use wisdom in discerning what messages are truly from the Lord, and we have three sources upon which to draw. First, the Holy Spirit will say nothing which contradicts the eternal Word. The Bible is our first source of judgment. Second, we have pastors and elders who are mature in the Lord and can give counsel in discerning whether or not a message truly originates from the Spirit. Finally, the same Holy Spirit dwells in us. If He is giving a message to the Church or to you personally, He can bear witness to it in your own spirit.

The second way this error may have arisen was "by word." False teaching was alive in the Church from the beginning, and it is still alive today. To combat false teaching, we must know the Bible—it is the foundation of our doctrine. However, we must also interpret the Bible rightly. An important factor in proper interpretation that has been long overlooked in Protestant circles is interpreting the Word within a body of believers. We need the Body of Christ to help balance our interpretation of the Word. I believe much of liberal Protestant theology would not have originated if the theologians had not been separated from the rank and file of the Body and left to do theology in a sterile academic setting. We need to have the balance provided by relationship with the Body because our life in Christ is a relationship, not merely an intellectual exercise.

Finally, error can come from "letter[s], as if from us." This is related to the previous point, but I want to focus on false teachers rather than false teaching. Today there are many who claim to be spiritual teachers. These teachers claim to have some source of authority which gives them the privilege to advise others on the proper way of life or the way to God. Once again our best defense is to be grounded in the Truth, and the way to be grounded in Truth is to be in the Word and the Body. Reading the Bible and regular fellowship with other believers will go a long way toward maintaining your walk with God. [157]

Time Management
Time management (though the term is a clichés, these days) is another of those things that can trip us up before we've begin our day. There are generally accepted rules of conduct and also specific personality traits – be yourself. If you are an early riser be that, but make sure you are aware of the needs of those around you and their expectations.

Alleine's Alarm

While a chaplain at Oxford, Joseph Alleine often neglected his friends for his studies. "It is better they should wonder at my rudeness," he explained, "than that I should lose time; for only a few will notice the rudeness, but many will feel my loss of time."Though barely 21, he was already "infinitely and insatiably greedy for the conversion of souls," devoting every moment to studying, preaching, and evangelizing. In 1655 Joseph was called to a Church in the west of England. He soon married, and his wife, Theodosia, later claimed his only fault was not spending more time with her. "Ah, my dear," he would say, "I know thy soul is safe; but how many that are perishing have I to look after?"

Joseph habitually rose at 4:00 in the morning, praying and studying his Bible until 8:00. His afternoons were spent calling on the unconverted. He kept a list of the inhabitants of each street and knew the condition of each soul. "Give me a Christian that counts his time more precious than gold," he said. At the beginning of the week, he would remark, "Another week is now before us, let us spend this week for God." Each morning he said, "Now let us live this one day well!"

But his time was nonetheless cut short. The restoration of England's monarchy in 1662 resulted in the Act of Uniformity, removing 2,000 preachers from their pulpits in a single day. Most preached their farewell sermons August 17, 1662. Joseph, however, continued preaching. The authorities descended, and on May 28, 1663 he was thrown into prison. His health soon declined.

"Now we have one day more," he told Theodosia when he was finally released. "Let us live well, work hard for souls, lay up much treasure in heaven this day, for we have but a few to live." He spoke truthfully. He died on November 17, 1668, at age 34. But he had spent his years well, outliving himself not only in the souls he saved, but in the book he left, a Puritan classic entitled Alleine's Alarm. [158]

Man of Habit
William Romaine was a safe and predictable minister in eighteenth-century England—until he sat under the preaching of George Whitefield. For the rest of his life, Romaine was a fiery evangelical in the Church of England. His zeal confounded Church leaders, and he lost both friends and positions. In at least one Church, officials refused to light the building where he spoke, forcing him to

preach by the light of a single candle held in his hand. But Romaine's revivalistic preaching drew larger and larger audiences until all of London was affected.

While Whitefield traveled around the world and Wesley throughout Britain, Romaine held down the fort in London. That was his citadel, and he became the rallying point for London's Anglicans who loved the evangelical truth.

Romaine was a man of habit. He took breakfast each day at six, reading from the book of Psalms as he ate. Dinner was at half-past one, supper at seven in the evening, after which he took a walk. He conducted family prayer at nine in the morning and at nine at night. Bedtime was ten.

He lived to be 81, working unabated until his final illness. On Saturday, July 25, 1795, Romaine found himself unable to go down the stairs. He settled on an upstairs couch in great weakness, "giving glory to God." In late afternoon, he was heard to whisper, "Though I walk through the valley of the shadow of death I will fear no evil, for thou art with me." A little later, a friend bent over and said, "I hope, my dear sir, you now find the salvation of Jesus Christ precious, dear, and valuable to you." Romaine replied, "He is a precious Savior to me now." A little later, as though seeing the Lord, he cried, "Holy! Holy! Holy! Blessed Jesus! To thee be endless praise." And about midnight "as the Sabbath began" he took his final breath. His friends planned a private funeral, but thousands showed up. Fifty coaches followed the hearse, and multitudes on foot. His critics had long since folded their tents. The city loved him, and it loved his truth.[159]

Vision

Along with the need for goals and prophecies, comes the need for vision. The Lord is determined we write **the Word down so we have it to hold on to when we are weary.**

Proverbs 29:18,
> [18] Where *there is* no revelation, the people cast off restraint;
> But happy *is* he who keeps the law.[160]

Habakkuk 2:2-4,
> [2] Then the Lord answered me and said:
> "Write the vision
> And make *it* plain on tablets,
> That he may run who reads it.
>
> [3] For the vision *is* yet for an appointed time;
> But at the end it will speak, and it will not lie.
> Though it tarries, wait for it;
> Because it will surely come,
> It will not tarry.
>
> [4] "Behold the proud,
> His soul is not upright in him;
> But the just shall live by his faith.[161]

Dr. CLARE ERNSTZEN

The following is extracted from Frank Damazio's book, *The Making of a Leader*: [162]

We will now list some of the major causes of ministerial and spiritual digression (i.e. a turning aside from the progression or advancement toward one's goal) in a leader's life. The left-hand column lists attitudes that will cause a leader to progress. The right-hand column lists attitudes that will cause a leader to digress.

Progression	Digression
A teachable attitude keeps a leader open to following after God's wisdom and understanding. (Proverbs 2:1-5)	A hardened attitude in a leader prevents him from feeling the conviction of the Holy Spirit. Being too rigid and unyielding stops a leader's growth. (Mark 8:17)
A patient attitude endures hardship and allows God to accomplish His perfect will through the circumstances.	An impatient attitude causes a leader to make demands on God in a selfish way.
A forgiving attitude allows a leader to be emotionally free toward every person who may hurt him. (Matthew 6:14; Mark 11:25; Luke 17:4; Ephesians 4:32)	A critical attitude puts a leader into such a bondage of negativism and unbelief that a root of bitterness can easily be developed.
A blameless character and attitude allows a leader to move forward in the will of God. (II Corinthians 3:18)	A defective character or attitude eventually causes a leader to stumble and fall.
A single eye prevents a leader from swerving from his goal of serving God in his ministry. (Matthew 6:22)	A double minded leader will be unstable in all of his ways and not be able to lead the people clearly.
A persistent attitude enables a leader to rise again and again after	A discouraged attitude causes a leader self-centeredly to think

falling.	that he is the only one suffering such terrible problems in the kingdom.
A confident attitude, that a leader is called by God to do a special work in the kingdom, enables him to endure much opposition.	A doubtful attitude about a leader's call and place in the kingdom leads him to think that everyone else can do his task better than he can do it.
A co-operative attitude towards others' ministries opens a leader's heart to receive much from others.	A competitive attitude towards others' ministries closes a leader's heart from receiving anything from them.
A diligent attitude enables a leader to accomplish twice as much as he thought he could in the first place.	A slothful attitude make a leader waste a lot of the precious time that God has given to him to steward.
A loving attitude grants a leader the ability to be free from selfish frustration, as he gives himself freely to helping others.	An unloving attitude permits a leader's life to close in around him and makes him bitter, angry, selfish and frustrated.
A healing and forgiving attitude allows a leader to forgive and forget the past failures of his own and others.	A recollecting attitude puts a leader in bondage by constantly bringing to his mind his past failures as well as others.
An understanding attitude allows a leader to see God's eternal purposes in everything that happens to him in life.	A non-discerning attitude leads a man of God to inaccurate interpretations of the facts of his life.
A trusting and submissive attitude permits a leader to benefit from other leaders' counsel as he yields to their wisdom.	An overly-confident attitude will lead a ministry to be separated from his brethren and possibly fall into error without a multitude of counsellors. (Proverbs 15:22)

A patient attitude in a leader enables him to rest in the Lord since he chooses not to force God to move on his behalf.	An impatient attitude in a leader is when he refuses to see the value of time delays and causes him to miss the valuable insights that God has for him during such times.
A disciplined attitude in the study, prayer, and scheduling habits of a leader allows him to produce much fruit for the kingdom.	An undisciplined attitude leads a man of God to waste his time, money and energy on less valuable activities.
A positive attitude, which causes a leader to look for the good in other people, spiritually revolutionises all of his attitudes towards people.	A negative and critical attitude, which causes a leader to look for the bad in other people, binds his spirit in such a way that the love of God cannot flow through him.
A faithful attitude, which enables a leader to be loyal to God and to others even in the face of adversity, will be rewarded by God.	An inconsistent attitude, which causes a leader to quit when things get rough, spreads in every area of his life until he is no longer a dependable person even in the less important areas of life.
A transparent attitude, which enables a leader to rid his life of all bad habits (e.g. backbiting, procrastinating, being late) enables a man of God to grow consistently in his spiritual walk.	A non-transparent attitude, which permits a leader to cover-up all of his bad habits with self-justifications, does not allow him consistently to mature in the Lord.
A sensitive attitude, which enables a leader to discern the true feelings of those around him, gives him more effectiveness in ministering to the needs of others.	An insensitive attitude, which causes a leader to be aware only of his own thoughts and feelings and not those of others, decreases the effectiveness that he has in ministering to the needs of others.

A concerned attitude, which equips the leader with the ability to pay close attention to whatever is happening around him, causes people to respond to him more genuinely and more frequently.	An indifferent attitude, which causes a leader not to care about the people or his work, short circuits the effectiveness in his ministry.
A humble attitude, which is a realistic and modest sense of one's own abilities and importance, enables a leader to hear from the Lord. (Matthew 5:5; Philippians 2:3; I Peter 5:6)	A proud attitude, which is an overestimation of one's own abilities and importance, closes off a leader from hearing the Lord's voice and others from listening to him. (Proverbs 6:16, 17; 8:13)
A realistic attitude, which senses when a goal is possible, practical, and attainable, balances out the idealism of many leaders visions.	An unrealistic attitude, which centres on things that are not truthfully realisable, causes a leader to be constantly frustrated because what he sees is never what he wants to see.
A spiritual attitude, which causes a leader always to grow in his personal relationship with the Lord, enables him to broaden and deepen his ministry to others because he has something worth sharing from his own life.	A non-spiritual attitude, which is satisfied with the present extent of one's relationship with the Lord, lessens a leader's ability to reach others because he demonstrates no depth in his own spiritual experience with the Lord.
A friendly attitude, which takes the initiative to meet new people and make new friends, opens others' hearts to such a leader.	An unfriendly attitude, which does not care about anyone else except itself and its own clique of friends, closes people's hearts to such a leader.
A believing attitude, which trusts the Lord, His Word, and His work to be right, enables a leader to go from one level of faith to another in his life, seeing God respond to	A disrespectful attitude, which does not value the attitudes or life style of any other leader, isolates such a person inwardly from others because he thinks

him all the time that he believes Him.	that he has sufficient character in himself.
A non-comparative attitude, which accepts oneself as well as others as they are presently in God, frees such a leader from envy, jealousy, resentment, and strife because he does not lust after what someone else has or does.	A comparative attitude, which sizes up what one leader has or does with what another has or does, leads a man of God into a life of envy and bitterness because he is never content with what he has and never thanks God for what He has given to another.
A meek attitude, which recognises the extent and limitations of one's own ministry and gifts, enables a leader to know his need for other brethren because he does not think he is a one-man band ministry.	A presumptuous attitude, which does not recognise any weakness or limit to one's abilities in God, causes a leader to be cut off from his brethren because he believes that God has given him everything.
A sonship attitude, which openly recognises that at times a leader will need to be corrected by God, keeps a leader in an open and free relationship with his heavenly Father. (Hebrews 12:1ff)	A non-sonship attitude, which thinks that a leader never needs to be corrected by anyone because he is a leader, closes off such a leader's relationship to God as his Father.
A visionary attitude, which sees by faith beyond the present circumstances to the good that God wants to accomplish in the future, keeps a leader following the Lord with a strong faith.	A non-visionary attitude, which takes on the feelings of a fatalist: "What will be, will be", decreases a leader's ability to see beyond the present to what God wants to do in the Church in the future.
An open attitude, which realises one's need for counsel from the brethren, increases a leader's wisdom and understanding because he is making himself available to learn from others' knowledge and experience.	A closed attitude, which thinks that one does not need anyone else's counsel, decreases a leader's wisdom and understanding because he is not making himself available to learn from others' knowledge and experience.

A trainable attitude, which sees the need of relating to those in the ministry who are mature, broadens a leader's perspective of people and ministry.	A non-trainable attitude, which feels that there is no need to be linked with older ministries, cuts a leader off from valuable insights.
An organised attitude, which properly schedules one's time, increases a leader's time for serving the Lord.	A non-organised attitude, which puts no framework on the use of one's time, wastes many opportunities for helping people and serving the Lord.
A balanced attitude, which recognises the proper place of the various activities which God has given a leader to do, enables him to lead a happy and fulfilled life.	An imbalanced attitude, which does not give a rightful place to the different responsibilities of a leader, causes him to be frustrated and unfulfilled because of not allowing God to develop him in a well rounded way: spirit, mind, emotional and body.
A listening attitude, which hears not only what people are saying but also what they are not and cannot say, enables a leader to counsel more effectively to people who have deep wounds.	A non-listening attitude, which does not care to take the time to listen to anyone's problems or joys, cuts off a leader's effectiveness in trying to minister to others because others do not feel that such a leader is genuinely interested in them.
A restrained attitude, which allows a leader to speak in wisdom, propriety, and edification, enables people to respect such a man of God who would control his tongue. (James 3:1,2; I Timothy 3:8; Matthew 20:25,26; Philippians 1:15)	An unrestrained attitude, which permits a leader to say anything he wants to at anytime, decreases the peoples respect for him and his counsel. (Ecclesiastes 5:3)
An objective attitude, which puts	A subjective attitude, which laces

the clear standards of the Word of God above a leader's personal feelings; causes such a person to live an upright life and to be a good example for others to follow. (Genesis 22:1-13; Psalm 32:8)	a leader's own personal whims above the mandates of the Word of God, causes a man of God to fall into pure subjectivisms, rationalisations, and justifications of his own behaviour. (Numbers 22:9-20)
A sober attitude, which recognises the differences between healthy humour and jesting, causes a leader to know how to relate properly to all people on all levels.	A jesting attitude, which is a spirit of constant teasing: sarcasm and cynicism toward the character or unchangeable parts of a person's life, causes people to loose respect for a leader that has such an attitude.
A motivated attitude, which enables a leader to be self-starter and one that takes initiative in spiritual projects, enables him to accomplish good goals for the kingdom.	An unmotivated attitude, which causes a leader to be lazy and slow in all areas of his life, not only makes God feel unhappy, but also himself because of his lack of spiritual and natural accomplishment.
A resilient attitude, which is able to withstand the emotional jar from criticism or disagreement, enables a leader to keep strong (and yet tender) before the Lord and other people.	An overly-sensitive attitude, which is hurt / shocked by criticism or disagreement, cripples a leader emotionally, mentally, and spiritually because he takes everything that he hears in a very personal way.
A followable attitude, which causes people for different reasons, to be willing to follow a certain leader, enables him to be able to guide them where God wants them to go.	A non-followable attitude, which causes people, for different reasons, not to be willing to follow a particular leader, disenables him to lead them anywhere.
A modest attitude which views the things in the world only as	A vain attitude, which puts its affections on the external things

means to the end of building God's kingdom, enables a leader to give his life (without a spirit of covetousness) to building the kingdom of God.	of this life, trips up a leader in his walk with God spiritually because it bends him to a spirit of materialism and covetousness.
A discreet attitude, which governs a leader's life through scriptural priorities, enables him to build the kingdom of God and not the kingdom of this world.	An indiscreet attitude, which does not maintain Scriptural priorities, causes a leader to digress out of the will of God.
A steady attitude, which causes a leader to go into things at an even pace and not unwisely or too soon, keeps a leader from making unwise decisions which he may later regret.	A hasty attitude, which uses no wisdom in its desire to do things for God, causes a leader many hurt feelings, wrong decisions, and regrettable memories.
A conscientious attitude, which obeys the inner promptings of the Holy Spirit inside a leader's life, enables him to keep a pure conscience before God and man.	A neglectful attitude, which postpones obedience to the inner voice of the Holy Spirit in a leader's life, causes him not to be able to follow the Lord closely or hear what the Spirit is presently saying to the Church because his heart is too cluttered with unconfessed sins.
A decisive attitude, which enables a leader to make judgements appropriately without waiting too long, enables a leader to function as a good administrator over the house of the Lord.	An indecisive attitude, which waits too long in making important decisions, can put a leader or a Church into a bondage and fear of making a mistake, a lack of knowledge of the Word of God, a fear of man, and a spirit of perfectionism.
A courageous attitude, which gives strength to a leader when opposition or contradiction hit	A fearful attitude, which is a painful feeling of apprehension over a possible danger, stops a

his life, permits a leader to continue a firm faith in God through all circumstances.	leader from doing all that God has for him to do. Such an attitude can be a fear of the future, failure, persecution, or what God might require of a person.
A studious attitude, which causes a leader to give his time to meditation and study of the Scripture, enables him to have a better ministry of feeding his sheep, teaching, preaching, and counselling because he has a better grasp of God's perspective on life.	A non-studious attitude, which prevents a leader from spending time and energy in the Word of God, leads a man of God into having a very shallow ministry of feeding the flock or giving them directions.
A free attitude, which enables a leader to enter into the presence of God with praise and worship, keeps his spirit free from guilt through confession of sin and the cleansing blood of Jesus.	A condemned attitude, which is an inward feeling of being constantly unable to enter into God's presence because of guilt, prevents a leader from being free in his spirit to minister to the Lord and to others.
An established attitude, which a leader has when he knows how his daily life measures up against the Word of God, gives him a solid foundation upon which to rest when trials and temptations come his way.	An unestablished attitude, which a leader has when he does not know his place in Jesus Christ as a Christian, causes him to be unstable about basic doctrine, counsel to others, and in his daily walk with God.
An uncompromising attitude, which a leader has when he knows where he stands on basic issues in the Word of God, provides a great strength to the people who follow his leadership.	A compromising attitude, which is unsettled on basic Christian issues, gives a great feeling of instability and inferiority to the people of God because they do not know what to believe or why to believe it.
A sacrificing attitude, which a	A hypocritical attitude, which

leader has when he puts every aspect of his life at the disposal of Jesus Christ, enables him to be greatly used by God in his ministry because God's Spirit works through brokenness.	a leader has when he does not submit every area of his own life to Jesus Christ but continues to preach that others should, eventually leads his ministry to being very hollow and ineffective because the real life of the Holy Spirit is not flowing in and through it.

CHAPTER 10
INTERCESSION AND THE SERVANT'S HEART

Intercession and the servant's heart are almost synonymous. There will be many times when we are required to intercede on behalf of a fellow minister, a friend, a family member, or even as in the case of Rees Howell, for the world as a whole during times of war.

Principles of Intercession by Rees Howells:
- Identification.
- As the crucifix of self proceeds, intercession begins.
- The Holy Spirit can take the Intercessor into extremes to fulfil the intercession like Isaiah, Jeremiah, Ezekiel and Hosea, who are some of the great intercessors of the Bible.
- Agony in intercession. "if it dies, it brings forth much fruit" – Jesus.
- Authority. The intercessor finds a place of prevailing prayer with God.
- The gained position of intercession can be used in other prayer situations.
- Entering the "grace of faith". The measureless realms of God's grace are open for the intercessor to prevail upon.

More teaching from Rees Howell's College about intercession
- God gives you a prayer that you are responsible to pray through.
- When the Lord shows you the prayer, you are committed to it whatever the cost is and for however long it takes.
- Intercession is completely voluntary. You are never forced into prayer. The intercessor needs to be willing to enter into a new place of intercession.
- The intercessors love God so much that they want to obey. They will pay the price because of their love for the Saviour.
- The intercessors will discover wave upon wave of evil as they prevail upon God to see the spiritual systems that have held millions of people in bondage for centuries broken.
- There is death involved in intercession. But the focus is never just death. The Spirit of God is gaining ground all the time. You will gain tremendous power over the enemy.
- Intercession in many ways is hidden. The world does not see the prayer until it is completed. Jesus, the Intercessor, was misunderstood in His Intercession. Not until after the resurrection did the disciples begin to understand why He came. Only after His ascension did they begin to understand His work as the great

High Priest who entered into death to destroy it.

Isaiah 53:12,
>¹² Therefore I will divide Him a portion with the great,
>And He shall divide the spoil with the strong,
>Because He poured out His soul unto death,
>And He was numbered with the transgressors,
>And He bore the sin of many,
>And made intercession for the transgressors.[163]

INTERCESSION – the act of petitioning God or praying on behalf of another person or group. The sinful nature of this world separates human beings from God. It has always been necessary, therefore, for righteous individuals to go before God to seek reconciliation between Him and His fallen creation.

Examples of intercession occur in classic instances. In genesis 18, where Abraham speaks to God on behalf of Sodom, his plea ois compassionate; it is cocenred with the well-being of others rather than with his own needs. Such selfless concern is the mark of all true intercession.

Moses was also effective in petitioning God on behalf of the Hebrew people (Ex. 15:25). Even the pharaoh asked Moses to intercede for him (Ex. 8:28). But just as righteous men often succeeded in reconciling Creator and creation, the bible also reminds us that the ongoing sinfulness of a people can hinder the effects of intercession (1 Sam. 2:25; Jer. 7:16).

The sacrifices and prayers of Old Testament priests (Ex. 29:42; 30:7) were acts of intercession which point forward to the work of Christ. Christ is, of course, the greatest intercessor. he prayed on behalf of Peter (luke 22:32) and His disciples (John 17). Then in the most selfless intercession of all, He petitioned God on behalf of those who criucified Him (Luke 23:34). His work on the cross is His ultimate expression of intercession (Is. 53:12).

Christ's intercessionary work did not cease when He returned to heaven. He still intercedes for His Church (Heb. 7:25), and the Holy Spirit pleads on behalf of the individual Christian (Rom. 8:26-27). Finally because of their unique relationship to God through chrsist, Chrostoans are urged to intercede for all people (1 Tim. 2:1). The latter text shows intercessory prayer is a primary ministry of the Church.[164]

INTERCESSION. (Heb. 7:25) *entunchano* (en-toong-khan-oh); *Strongs #1793:* To fall in with, meet with an order to converse. From this description of a casual encounter, the word progresses to the idea of pleading with another person of behalf of another, although a times the petition may be against another (Acts 25:24; Rom. 11:2).[165]

INTERCESSION (MAKE). (Jer. 27:18) *paga'* (pah-gah); *Strong's #6293*: To reach, to meet someone; to pressure or urge someone strongly; to meet up with a person; encounter, entreat; to assail with urgent petitions. this verb occurs forty-six times. In some passages it is translated "meet," as in Joshua 2:16. In Joshua 19:27, *paga'* refers to the extent to which a tribal boundary is reached. Sometimes the verb refers to "falling upon" someone in battle, that is, to meet up with the enemy with hostile intent (1 Kin. 2:29). *Paga'* is also translated "make intercession," the idea being that a supplicant catches up with a superior, and reaches him with an urgent request. Thus, intercession involves reaching God, meeting God, and entresting Him for His favor.[166]

1 Timothy 2:1-4,

Therefore I exhort first of all that supplications, prayers, intercessions, *and* giving of thanks be made for all men, ² for kings and all who are in authority, that we may lead a quiet and peaceable life in all godliness and reverence. ³ For this *is* good and acceptable in the sight of God our Savior, ⁴ who desires all men to be saved and to come to the knowledge of the truth.[167]

Ezekiel 22:30,

³⁰ So I sought for a man among them who would make a wall, and stand in the gap before Me on behalf of the land, that I should not destroy it; but I found no one.[168]

Gap, *perets.* A break, gap, or breach; especially a gap in a wall. *Perets* comes from the verb *parats*, "to break forth, break open, or break down." Two verses (Is. 58:12; Amos 9:11) show that gaps or breaches need to be repaired; the former verse refers o the physical and spiritual ruins of Zion, and the latter to the tabernacle of David. In Ezekiel 22;30, "standing in the gap" is a metaphor for committed intercession. This refers to the gap between God and man that an intercessor tries to repair.[169]

Isaiah 58:12,
¹² Those from among you
Shall build the old waste places;
You shall raise up the foundations of many generations;
And you shall be called the Repairer of the Breach,
The Restorer of Streets to Dwell In.[170]

Romans 8:26-28,

²⁶ Likewise the Spirit also helps in our weaknesses. For we do not know what we should pray for as we ought, but the Spirit Himself makes intercession for us with groanings which cannot be uttered. ²⁷ Now He who searches the hearts knows what the mind of the Spirit *is,* because He makes intercession for the saints according to *the will of* God. ²⁸ And we know that all things work together for good to those who love God, to those who are the called according to *His* purpose.[171]

Hebrews 7:24-25,

²⁴ But He, because He continues forever, has an unchangeable priesthood. ²⁵ Therefore He is also able to save to the uttermost those who come to God through Him, since He always lives to make intercession for them.[172]

Example 1: Abraham intercedes for Sodom and Gomorrah (Gen. 18:17-33)
Example 2: Moses intercedes for Israel (Ex.32:31-35; 33:7-14)
Example 3: David intercedes for his son (2 Sam. 12:13-23)
Example 4: Daniel intercedes for Israel (Dan. 9:1-9)[173]

CHAPTER 11
BIBLICAL EXAMPLES OF SERVANT LEADERSHIP

The following is a list of some leaders in the Old Testament who were definitely servants of God and others:

1. Abraham: God's servant (Genesis 26:24)
2. Moses: God's servant (Exodus 14:31; Numbers 12:7-8; Deuteronomy 34:5; Joshua 1:1,2,7)
3. Joshua: Moses' servant (Exodus 33:11)
4. Caleb: God's servant (Numbers 14:24)
5. Samuel: God's servant (1 Samuel 3:9)
6. David: Saul's servant (1 Samuel 29;3)
   God's servant (1 Chronicles 17:4)
7. Elijah: God's servant (II Kings 9:36)
8. Nehemiah: God's servant (Nehemiah 1:6)
9. Isaiah: God's servant (Isaiah 20:2)

Jesus
Perhaps the most amazing object lesson of servant leadership was when Jesus washed His disciples' feet. This ritual was definitely one for the lower of the slaves, a menial task necessitated by the dust of the roads and the types of sandals worn during that time. There being much use of animals on the roads, also led to the feet needing cleansing.

John 13:1-17,
Now before the Feast of the Passover, when Jesus knew that His hour had come that He should depart from this world to the Father, having loved His own who were in the world, He loved them to the end. [2] And supper being ended, the devil having already put it into the heart of Judas Iscariot, Simon's *son,* to betray Him, [3] Jesus, knowing that the Father had given all things into His hands, and that He had come from God and was going to God, [4] rose from supper and laid aside His garments, took a towel and girded Himself. [5] After that, He poured water into a basin and began to wash the disciples' feet, and to wipe *them* with the towel with which He was girded. [6] Then He came to Simon Peter. And *Peter* said to Him, "Lord, are You washing my feet?" [7] Jesus answered and said to him, "What I am doing you do not understand now, but you will know after this." [8] Peter said to Him, "You shall never wash my feet!" Jesus answered him, "If

The Servant's Heart

I do not wash you, you have no part with Me." ⁹ Simon Peter said to Him, "Lord, not my feet only, but also *my* hands and *my* head!" ¹⁰ Jesus said to him, "He who is bathed needs only to wash *his* feet, but is completely clean; and you are clean, but not all of you." ¹¹ For He knew who would betray Him; therefore He said, "You are not all clean." ¹² So when He had washed their feet, taken His garments, and sat down again, He said to them, "Do you know what I have done to you? ¹³ You call Me Teacher and Lord, and you say well, for *so* I am. ¹⁴ If I then, *your* Lord and Teacher, have washed your feet, you also ought to wash one another's feet. ¹⁵ For I have given you an example, that you should do as I have done to you. ¹⁶ Most assuredly, I say to you, a servant is not greater than his master; nor is he who is sent greater than he who sent him. ¹⁷ If you know these things, blessed are you if you do them.[174]

When looking at this passage, the first verse that jumps at me is verse 3:
³ Jesus, knowing that the Father had given all things into His hands, and that He had come from God and was going to God,

When we as leaders, can stand firmly in this truth, there should be nothing that can take us out. In theory, we know we are going to heaven and thus will go to God, but has this really sunk into our hearts? When we get into Heaven, are we going in as a leader to be welcomed or are we going to try and sneak in through a back door?

As leaders we can sometimes try and hide our deep internal workings because we do not trust the people around us. Yes there is wisdom in keeping things close so that we are accountable to some, but there is also a danger in being so closed that we are not real to the people we are supposed to be leading.

In verse 5 we see that Jesus washed the disciples' feet with water, and had dried them with a towel. In the previous chapter, Jesus' own feet had been anointed with perfume by Mary.

John 12:1-3,

Then, six days before the Passover, Jesus came to Bethany, where Lazarus was who had been dead, whom He had raised from the dead. ² There they made Him a supper; and Martha served, but Lazarus was one of those who sat at the table with Him. ³ Then Mary took a pound of very costly oil of spikenard, anointed the feet of Jesus, and wiped His feet with her hair. And the house was filled with the fragrance of the oil.[175]

Vernon McGee says the following concerning the washing of the disciples' feet and the anointing of Jesus' feet:

In the preceding chapter, you will remember, we saw that the feet of Jesus were anointed. Here, the feet of the disciples are washed. What a difference! As the Savior passed through this sinful world, He contracted no defilement whatsoever. He was holy, harmless, and undefiled. The feet speak of the walk of a person, and the anointing of Jesus' feet with spikenard tells of the sweet savor of the *walk of our Lord.*

The disciples' feet needed washing! Jesus washed their feet with water, not with blood. That is important to see. ... The blood of Jesus Christ, God's Son, cleanses us from all sin—past, present, and future—in one application. There is only one sacrifice. "For by one offering he hath perfected for ever them that are sanctified" (Heb. 10:14). When you and I came as sinners to Christ Jesus, it was His shed blood that once and for all cleansed us and gave us a standing before God. But, my friend, we need to be purified along the pilgrim pathway; in our walk through the world we get dirty, and we need washing. We shall see that our Lord washed His disciples' feet for *this very definite purpose.*[176]

As leaders there will be times when we have to take on this kind of position, that of performing a seemingly menial task. For some we will have to assist with counselling a rebellious child, for others we will have to quietly pay bail or pay for Alcoholics Anonymous or some other addictive relief assistance. At this time we can expect some of our advances to be met with Peter's initial response of "You shall never wash my feet!" – "I will never let you pay for that." Yes, what we may offer might seem immediately inappropriate, but will really be of necessity in the long term.

Commentators agree that Jesus' response has symbolic significance; a significance that became clear only after His death and resurrection. Jesus said, "He who is bathed needs only to wash his feet, but is completely clean; and you are clean, but not all of you" (v. 10).
Jesus used two Greek words here for washing. The first, louo, rightly translated "bathed" in our text, was used of washing the entire body. The second, translated "wash" (nipto), indicated washing a part of the body.[177]

Sometimes our flock will need a helping hand or a 'hose down' to get the stains and the dust of the road off them so they can be refreshed and restored and move on. We too will need to set time aside to gently wash each of our peoples' feet and spend some quality time with each one, touching their sore parts, washing away words of condemnation, using a balm or hand cream to replenish their skin and spirits.

Nehemiah

In the Book of Nehemiah we read an account of a man who took on **a leadership role that surpassed many. Nehemiah heard** a report of the state of Jerusalem, and took the matter to God in prayer.

Nehemiah 1:1-11,

The words of Nehemiah the son of Hachaliah. t came to pass in the month of

Chislev, *in* the twentieth year, as I was in Shushan the citadel, **2** that Hanani one of my brethren came with men from Judah; and I asked them concerning the Jews who had escaped, who had survived the captivity, and concerning Jerusalem. **3** And they said to me, "The survivors who are left from the captivity in the province *are* there in great distress and reproach. The wall of Jerusalem *is* also broken down, and its gates are burned with fire." **4** So it was, when I heard these words, that I sat down and wept, and mourned *for many* days; I was fasting and praying before the God of heaven. **5** And I said: "I pray, Lord God of heaven, O great and awesome God, *You* who keep *Your* covenant and mercy with those who love You and observe Your commandments, **6** please let Your ear be attentive and Your eyes open, that You may hear the prayer of Your servant which I pray before You now, day and night, for the children of Israel Your servants, and confess the sins of the children of Israel which we have sinned against You. Both my father's house and I have sinned. **7** We have acted very corruptly against You, and have not kept the commandments, the statutes, nor the ordinances which You commanded Your servant Moses. **8** Remember, I pray, the word that You commanded Your servant Moses, saying, '*If* you are unfaithful, I will scatter you among the nations; **9** but *if* you return to Me, and keep My commandments and do them, though some of you were cast out to the farthest part of the heavens, *yet* I will gather them from there, and bring them to the place which I have chosen as a dwelling for My name.' **10** Now these *are* Your servants and Your people, whom You have redeemed by Your great power, and by Your strong hand. **11** O Lord, I pray, please let Your ear be attentive to the prayer of Your servant, and to the prayer of Your servants who desire to fear Your name; and let Your servant prosper this day, I pray, and grant him mercy in the sight of this man." For I was the king's cupbearer.[178]

Now in those days, an unwalled city was considered beneath contempt. Nehemiah's heart broke with the perceived contempt for the holy city, and he immediately took this problem to the Lord in prayer and fasting. Many times a leader will find himself in this position. There is no substitute for the prayer and fasting life of a dedicated leader before God.

Nehemiah did not consider himself and his family above the disgrace that Israel had become and immediately included himself in his prayer of repentance. There will be times as leaders we need to accept responsibility for the actions of others – seeing as we reap their consequences as well!

Nehemiah was so convicted about the state of the city of Jerusalem, that he requested permission to be made governor of Jerusalem and set in charge of rebuilding the walls.

Nehemiah 2:4-6,

4 Then the king said to me, "What do you request?" So I prayed to the God of heaven. ⁵ And I said to the king, "If it pleases the king, and if your servant has found favor in your sight, I ask that you send me to Judah, to the city of my fathers' tombs, that I may rebuild it." ⁶ Then the king said to me (the queen also sitting beside him), "How long will your journey be? And when will you return?" So it pleased the king to send me; and I set him a time.[179]

There will be times when, as leaders, we will have been given a vision of what the Lord has asked us to do, and He will open doors to enable us to accomplish what He has set before us, but it will not be an easy task. Like Nehemiah, we will encounter those who verbally support us but backlash us, amd those who downright rebel against everything we suggest.

Nehemiah 2:17-20,

¹⁷ Then I said to them, "You see the distress that we *are* in, how Jerusalem *lies* waste, and its gates are burned with fire. Come and let us build the wall of Jerusalem, that we may no longer be a reproach." ¹⁸ And I told them of the hand of my God which had been good upon me, and also of the king's words that he had spoken to me. So they said, "Let us rise up and build." Then they set their hands to *this* good *work.* ¹⁹ But when Sanballat the Horonite, Tobiah the Ammonite official, and Geshem the Arab heard *of it,* they laughed at us and despised us, and said, "What *is* this thing that you are doing? Will you rebel against the king?" ²⁰ So I answered them, and said to them, "The God of heaven Himself will prosper us; therefore we His servants will arise and build, but you have no heritage or right or memorial in Jerusalem."[180]

Nehemiah 4:7-8,

⁷ Now it happened, when Sanballat, Tobiah, the Arabs, the Ammonites, and the Ashdodites heard that the walls of Jerusalem were being restored and the gaps were beginning to be closed, that they became very angry, ⁸ and all of them conspired together to come *and* attack Jerusalem and create confusion.[181]

With the building programme eventually off the floor, Nehemiah became aware of some distinctly unimpressive money changing going on amongst his people. The people were falling deeper and deeper into debt because of the famine while they were assisting with the rebuilding of Jerusalem's wall.

Note from verse 6 and verse 7 that Nehemiah became angry – BUT he managed to think seriously about the situation before reacting.

Nehemiah 5:1-13,
And there was a great outcry of the people and their wives against their Jewish

brethren. ² For there were those who said, "We, our sons, and our daughters *are* many; therefore let us get grain, that we may eat and live." ³ There were also *some* who said, "We have mortgaged our lands and vineyards and houses, that we might buy grain because of the famine." ⁴ There were also those who said, "We have borrowed money for the king's tax *on* our lands and vineyards. ⁵ Yet now our flesh *is* as the flesh of our brethren, our children as their children; and indeed we are forcing our sons and our daughters to be slaves, and *some* of our daughters have been brought into slavery. *It is* not in our power *to redeem them,* for other men have our lands and vineyards." ⁶ And I became very angry when I heard their outcry and these words. ⁷ After serious thought, I rebuked the nobles and rulers, and said to them, "Each of you is exacting usury from his brother." So I called a great assembly against them. ⁸ And I said to them, "According to our ability we have redeemed our Jewish brethren who were sold to the nations. Now indeed, will you even sell your brethren? Or should they be sold to us?" Then they were silenced and found nothing *to say.* ⁹ Then I said, "What you are doing *is* not good. Should you not walk in the fear of our God because of the reproach of the nations, our enemies? ¹⁰ I also, *with* my brethren and my servants, am lending them money and grain. Please, let us stop this usury! ¹¹ Restore now to them, even this day, their lands, their vineyards, their olive groves, and their houses, also a hundredth of the money and the grain, the new wine and the oil, that you have charged them." ¹² So they said, "We will restore *it,* and will require nothing from them; we will do as you say." Then I called the priests, and required an oath from them that they would do according to this promise. ¹³ Then I shook out the fold of my garment and said, "So may God shake out each man from his house, and from his property, who does not perform this promise. Even thus may he be shaken out and emptied." And all the assembly said, "Amen!" and praised the Lord. Then the people did according to this promise.[182]

Nehemiah did not take any remuneration from the people for the entire 12 years it took to rebuild the wall. As leaders we will sometimes be called to walk by faith in the area of finances. This is not the time to develop 'hint faith'. Many Christians see this as a kind of 'stand with me and believe for the following' when really all they are doing is hinting in the vain (hopefully) hope that someone will provide for their desires – not their needs.

As leaders there is an area you will be called on to act as the Hand of God and supply the needs of your people; but always remember you do this in the strength of the Lord – don't do what Moses did, and when told to speak the rock, hit it.

Numbers 20:7-12,

⁷ Then the Lord spoke to Moses, saying, ⁸ "Take the rod; you and your brother

Aaron gather the congregation together. Speak to the rock before their eyes, and it will yield its water; thus you shall bring water for them out of the rock, and give drink to the congregation and their animals." [9] So Moses took the rod from before the Lord as He commanded him. [10] And Moses and Aaron gathered the assembly together before the rock; and he said to them, "Hear now, you rebels! Must we bring water for you out of this rock?" [11] Then Moses lifted his hand and struck the rock twice with his rod; and water came out abundantly, and the congregation and their animals drank. [12] Then the Lord spoke to Moses and Aaron, "Because you did not believe Me, to hallow Me in the eyes of the children of Israel, therefore you shall not bring this assembly into the land which I have given them."[183]

Nehemiah 5:14-18,

[14] Moreover, from the time that I was appointed to be their governor in the land of Judah, from the twentieth year until the thirty-second year of King Artaxerxes, twelve years, neither I nor my brothers ate the governor's provisions. [15] But the former governors who *were* before me laid burdens on the people, and took from them bread and wine, besides forty shekels of silver. Yes, even their servants bore rule over the people, but I did not do so, because of the fear of God. [16] Indeed, I also continued the work on this wall, and we did not buy any land. All my servants *were* gathered there for the work. [17] And at my table *were* one hundred and fifty Jews and rulers, besides those who came to us from the nations around us. [18] Now *that* which was prepared daily *was* one ox *and* six choice sheep. Also fowl were prepared for me, and once every ten days an abundance of all kinds of wine. Yet in spite of this I did not demand the governor's provisions, because the bondage was heavy on this people.[184]

We need to be especially careful of our reputations with regards to our physical appetites – it can be too easy when a ministry is doing well to allow ourselves luxuries that we have been forced to forego and suddenly we start tapping the ministry to fulfil our appetites. Nehemiah gave the perfect example of self control – for twelve years!

Nehemiah is also well known for his teaching of the Law to the people who had returned to live in the City of Jerusalem. His instruction led to the celebration of the Feast of Tabernacles for the first time since the days of Joshua. We need to msake certain our people are well versed in the Scriptures, as we will be held accountable for them.

Nehemiah 8:8,

So they read distinctly from the book, in the Law of God; and they gave the sense, and helped them to understand the reading.[185]

The following précis of Nehemiah's leadership skills is found in *Every man in the Bible*:

Nehemiah is rightly honored for his strong spiritual and political leadership. From Nehemiah we learn that to be effective leaders, we need to:
- *Become aware of a need, pray about it, and form a vision for meeting the need. Frequently those who form such a vision will be called by God to fulfill it.*
- *Commit ourselves to the vision God gives us. Often we may have to set aside other perfectly valid concerns and give ourselves to carrying out the vision given by God.*
- *Share our vision with others. One test for the validity of a vision is our ability to form a team of others motivated to see that the vision is carried out.*
- *Persist in our efforts to fulfill the vision should opposition develop. Satan has an active interest in thwarting God's purposes, so that opposition should not be unexpected.*
- *Provide a personal example of dedication to the vision, bearing the burden of any personal sacrifices that may be called for.*
- *Demonstrate a concern that all involved in the enterprise maintain a close personal relationship with God. God is to be honored in the workers as well as in the work.* [186]

CHAPTER 12
CONCLUSION

In conclusion, we see whilst we are not to be a legalistic people set on works for the Lord, we cannot experience the fullness of a relationship with Him, unless we have received the change of heart that separates us from the world.

Without a servant's heart, we can be guilty of grieving the Holy Spirit, as we fail to walk in God's desired plan for our lives. The softness of the servant's heart allows us to hear the Voice of the Lord in a new and more intimate way.

The servant's heart removes all thoughts of self, all selfish motives, all pagan rituals, all religious activities, and sets us at the Feet of our Lord, with ears that hear, eyes that see, and hearts that are soft and pliable in the Father's Hands.

The servant's heart is not an abstract description of ethereal qualities, but is a tangible evidence available to each one as we submit to the Lord, and trust Him to complete the good work He has begun in us.

Unless each believer accepts the command of the Lord to undergo this kind of heart change, their lives will remain unchanged, their hearts hardened, and may possibly have to endure the rebuke for the hardness of their hearts as did the disciples in

Mark 16;14,
> [14] Later He appeared to the eleven as they sat at the table; and He rebuked their unbelief and hardness of heart, because they did not believe those who had seen Him after He had risen.[187]

> Would we not rather hear the words, "Well done good and faithful servant!"

BIBLIOGRAPHY

Bailey, Brian. 1995. The Comforter. U.S.A.: Zion Christian Publishers.
Bailey, Brian. 2004. Leadership. U.S.A.: Zion Christian Publishers.
Blackaby, H & R. 2001. Spiritual Leadership. U.S.A.: Broadman & Holman Publishers.
Caram, Paul G. 1993. Turning the Curse into a Blessing. U.S.A.: Zion Christian Publishers.
Damazio, F. 1980. The Making of a Leader. U.S.A.: Bible Temple Inc.
Daniel, D. 2005. Biblical Leadership. R.S.A.: Creda Communications.
Enyagu, G. Hunter, M. 1989. Pastor. Ghana: African Christian Press.
Fawcett, J.R. 1992. Prayer, Praise and Worship. R.S.A.: Hebron Ministries C.C.
Ford, G. 1964. Manual on Management for Christian Workers. U.S.A.: Zondervan Publishing House.
Ford, L. 1991. Transforming Leadership. U.S.A.: InterVarsity Press.
Grams, Betty Jane. 1978. Women of Grace. U.S.A.: Gospel Publishing House.
Green, Keith. 1993. A Cry in the Wilderness. U.K.: Nelson Word Ltd.
Grubb, Norman P. 1952. Rees Howells Intercessor. U.K.: W & J Mackay & Co.
Hayford, J. W., & Hayford, J. W. I. (1997, c1996). Fearless Faith : Standing firm in the Freedom and Hope: A study of Galatians, 1&2 Thessalonians. Spirit-Filled Life Bible Discovery Guides. Nashville: Thomas Nelson.
Hayford, J. W., & Hagan, K. A. (1997). Passing Faith's Tests with Love and Joy : A study of James, 1&2 Peter, 1-3 John, Jude. Spirit-Filled Life Bible Discovery Guides. Nashville: Thomas Nelson.
Hayford, J. W., & Van Cleave, N. (1997, c1993). God's Way to Wholeness : Divine Healing by the Power of the Holy Spirit. Spirit-Filled Life Kingdom Dynamics Study Guides. Nashville: Thomas Nelson.
Hayford, J. W., Howse, G., & Posey, M. (1997, c1996). Race and Reconciliation : Healing the Wounds, Winning the Harvest. Spirit-Filled Life Kingdom Dynamics Study Guides. Nashville: Thomas Nelson.
Hayford, J. W., & Snider, J. (1997, c1995). Twelve Voices for Truth : Confronting a Falling World with Hope: A Study of the Minor Prophets. Spirit-Filled Life Bible Discovery Guides. Nashville: Thomas Nelson.
Hurley, V. 2000. Speaker's sourcebook of new illustrations. Dallas: Word Publishers.

Hurnard, Hannah. 1993. Hinds feet in high places. U.S.A.: Tyndale House Publishers Inc.

Jenkins, D. 1967. The Gift of Ministry. U.K.: Latimer Trend & Co Ltd.

Johnson, D. Nash, D. 1958. The Discipline of Leadership. U.K.: Staples Printers Limited.

Kovacs, Aimee Verduzco. 1996. Dancing into the Anointing. U.S.A.: Destiny Image Publishers Ltd.

Kurian, G. T. 2001. Nelson's new Christian dictionary : The authoritative resource on the Christian world. Nashville, Tenn.: Thomas Nelson Pubs.

Landsman, Michael Dr. 1987. Attitude of a Servant. South Plainfield, New Jersey, U.S.A.: Bridge Publishing Inc.

Little, G. 1987. 101 Ways to be a Better Manager. Australia, Reed Methuen.

MacDonald, W., & Farstad, A. (1997, c1995). Believer's Bible Commentary : Old and New Testaments (Col 3:8). Nashville: Thomas Nelson.

McKellar, I. 1997. The Violins of Change. Singapore: Touch Ministries International.

Marshall, C. 1982. The Prayers of Peter Marshall (Grand Rapids, MI: Chosen Books,

Maxwell, John C. 1993. Developing the leader within you. U.S.A.: Injoy Inc.

Maxwell, John C. 2000. The 21 Most Powerful Minutes in a Leader's day. U.S.A.: Thomas Nelson Publishers.

Maxwell, John C. Parrott, L. 2005. 25 Ways to Win with People. U.S.A.: Thomas Nelson Publishers.

Maxwell, John C. 1997. Becoming a Person of Influence. U.S.A.: Thomas Nelson Publishers.

Maxwell, John C. 2001. Be a People Person. U.S.A.: Thomas Nelson Publishers.

Maxwell, John C. 1998. The 21 Irrefutable Laws of Leadership. U.S.A.: Thomas Nelson Publishers.

Maxwell, John C. 2001. The 17 Indisputable Laws of Teamwork. U.S.A.: Thomas Nelson Publishers.

Maxwell, John C. 1995. Developing the Leaders Around You. U.S.A.: Thomas Nelson Publishers.

McClung, Floyd. 1987. The Father Heart of God. U.S.A.: Kingsway Publications.

McGee, J. V. (1997, c1981). Thru the Bible commentary. Nashville: Thomas Nelson.

Maswanganyi, E. Connor, K. 2000. Biblical Principles of Leadership. R.S.A.: Hebron Theological College.

Maswanganyi, E. Dynamic Christian Leadership. R.S.A.: Spring Valley Press.

Morgan, R. J. (2000). Nelson's complete book of stories, illustrations, and quotes (electronic ed.) Nashville: Thomas Nelson Publishers.

Morgan, R. J. (2000, c1997). On this day : 265 amazing and inspiring stories about saints, martyrs & heroes (electronic ed.) (July 25). Nashville: Thomas Nelson Publishers

Murphy, E. F. (1997, c1996). Handbook for spiritual warfare. Nashville: Thomas Nelson.

Murray, Andrew. 1982. Humility. U.S.A.: Whitaker House.

Nee, Watchman. 1972. Spiritual Authority. U.S.A.: Christian Fellowship Publishers Inc.

Osei-Mensah, G. 1990. Wanted: Servant Leaders. Ghana: African Christian Press.

Padgett, N. 1957. The Beginner Leadership Manual. U.S.A.: Convention Press.

Prime, D. 1964. A Christian's Guide to Leadership. U.K.: Hodder and Stoughton.

Richards, L. 1999. Every man in the Bible (143). Nashville: T. Nelson.

Richards, L., Pegoda, D., & Gross, P. 2001 Every teaching of Jesus in the Bible. Nashville: T. Nelson.

Sheets, Dutch. 1996. Intercessory Prayer. California, U.S.A.: Regal Books.

Sheets, Dutch. 1998. River of God. California, U.S.A.: Regal Books.

Smith, W. 1997. Smith's Bible dictionary. Nashville: Thomas Nelson.

Thomas, W. Ian Major. 1967. If I perish I perish. U.S.A.: Zondervan Publishing House.

Vine, W. (1997, c1996). Collected writings of W.E. Vine. Nashville: Thomas Nelson.

Wardle, Terry. 1973. Exalt Him! U.S.A.: Christian Publications.

Wiersbe, W. W. 1997. With the word Bible commentary . Nashville: Thomas Nelson.

Witherington, Ben III. 1995. Conflict and Community in Corinth Grand Rapids: Eerdmans.

Zodhiates, Spiros. 1984. Hebrew-Greek Key Study Bible. U.S.A.: AMG International Inc.

The Amplified Bible. U.S.A.: Zondervan Corporation.

Dr. CLARE ERNSTZEN

The New International Bible. U.S.A.: Zondervan Corporation.
The New King James Version. Nashville: Thomas Nelson.
Oxford Dictionary. 1911. U.S.A.: Oxford University Press.
Leadership. Spring 1998. U.S.A.: Christianity Today.
Leadership. Summer 1999. U.S.A.: Christianity Today.
Leadership. Winter 2001. U.S.A.: Christianity Today.
HYPERLINK"http://www.leadershipnow.com/leadershipquotes.html"
http://www.leadershipnow.com/leadershipquotes.html
Kurian, G. T. (2001). Nelson's New Christian Dictionary : The authoritative resource on the Christian world. Nashville, Tenn.: Thomas Nelson Pubs.
Bailey, Brian. 1995. The Comforter. U.S.A.: Zion Christian Publishers.
Morgan, R. J. (2000). Nelson's complete book of stories, illustrations, and quotes (electronic ed.) (Page 245). Nashville: Thomas Nelson Publishers.
Morgan, R. J. (2000). Nelson's complete book of stories, illustrations, and quotes (electronic ed.) (Page 244). Nashville: Thomas Nelson Publishers.
Sheets, D. (1996) Intercessory Prayer. California U.S.A.: Regal Books.
The New King James Version. 1982 (Dt 8:18). Nashville: Thomas Nelson.
Caram, Paul G. 1993. Turning the curse into a blessing. U.S.A.: Zion Christian Publishers.
The New King James Version. 1982 (Is 55:8-9). Nashville: Thomas Nelson.
Nee, Watchman. 1972. Spiritual Authority. U.S.A.: Christian Fellowship Publishers Inc.
Smith, W. (1997). Smith's Bible dictionary. Nashville: Thomas Nelson.
Catherine Marshall, The Prayers of Peter Marshall (Grand Rapids, MI: Chosen Books, a division of Baker Book House Co., 1982), 45.
MacDonald, W., & Farstad, A. (1997, c1995). Believer's Bible Commentary : Old and New Testaments (Col 3:8). Nashville: Thomas Nelson.
Wiersbe, W. W. (1997, c1991).

---

[1] The New King James Version. 1996, c1982 (Mk 16;14). Nashville: Thomas Nelson

[2] Kurian, G.T. (2001). *Nelson's New Christian Dictionary : The authoritative resource on the Chrisatian world.* Nashville, Tenn.: Thomas Nelson Pubs

[3] The New King James Version. 1996, c1982 (Mt 23:11). Nashville: Thomas Nelson

[4] The New King James Version. 1996, c1982 (Is 42:1-4). Nashville: Thomas Nelson

[5] The New King James Version. 1996, c1982 (Is 49:1-6). Nashville: Thomas Nelson

[6] The New King James Version. 1996, c1982 (Is Is 50:4-9). Nashville: Thomas Nelson

[7] Bailey, B. 1995. *The Comforter. Pg 182* U.S.A. Zion Christian Publishers.

[8] The New King James Version. 1996, c1982 (Jn 3:16). Nashville: Thomas Nelson

[9] The New King James Version. 1996, c1982 (Jer 31:3). Nashville: Thomas Nelson

[10] The New King James Version. 1996, c1982 (Rom 5:8). Nashville: Thomas Nelson

[11] The New King James Version. 1996, c1982 (Jn 15:13). Nashville: Thomas Nelson

[12] The New King James Version. 1996, c1982 (Phil 2:6-11). Nashville: Thomas Nelson

[13] Morgan, R.J. (2000). *Nelson's Complete book of Stories, Illustrations, and Quotes* (electronic ed.) (Page 245). Nashville: Thomas Nelson Publishers

[14] Morgan, R.J. (2000). *Nelson's Complete book of Stories, Illustrations, and Quotes* (electronic ed.) (Page 245). Nashville: Thomas Nelson Publishers

[15] The New King James Version. 1996, c1982 (Ex 3:7-8). Nashville: Thomas Nelson

[16] Sheets, D. (1996) *Intercessory Prayer.* California U.S.A.: Regal Books

[17] Sheets, D. (1996) *Intercessory Prayer.* California U.S.A.: Regal Books

[18] The New King James Version. 1996, c1982 (1 Tim 2:5). Nashville: Thomas Nelson

[19] The New King James Version. 1996, c1982 (Deut 8:18). Nashville: Thomas Nelson

[20] Murray, Andrew. (1895) *Humility.* U.S.A.: Anson D. F. Randolph & Co

[21] *ibid.*

[22] Caram, Paul G. (1993) *Turning the Curse into a Blessing.* U.S.A.: Zion Christian Publishers

[23] The New King James Version. 1996, c1982 (Isa 55:8-9). Nashville: Thomas Nelson

[24] The New King James Version. 1996, c1982 (Ho 11:8-11). Nashville:

[25] The New King James Version. 1996, c1982 (Ho 11:3-4). Nashville: Thomas Nelson

[26] The New King James Version. 1996, c1982 (Ho 2:6-8). Nashville: Thomas Nelson

[27] The New King James Version. 1996, c1982 (Col 3:12-17). Nashville: Thomas Nelson

[28] The New King James Version. 1996, c1982 (Ps 51:1). Nashville: Thomas Nelson

[29] The New King James Version. 1996, c1982 (Ps 51:2). Nashville: Thomas Nelson

[30] The New King James Version. 1996, c1982 (Ps 51:3-4). Nashville: Thomas Nelson

[31] The New King James Version. 1996, c1982 (Ps 51:5-6). Nashville: Thomas Nelson

[32] The New King James Version. 1996, c1982 (Ps 51:7-9). Nashville: Thomas Nelson

[33] The New King James Version. 1996, c1982 (Ps 51:10). Nashville: Thomas Nelson

[34] The New King James Version. 1996, c1982 (Ez 36:26-27). Nashville: Thomas Nelson

[35] The New King James Version. 1996, c1982 (Ps 51:11). Nashville: Thomas Nelson

[36] The New King James Version. 1996, c1982 (Ps 51:12-14). Nashville: Thomas Nelson

[37] The New King James Version. 1996, c1982 (Ps 51:15). Nashville: Thomas Nelson

[38] The New King James Version. 1996, c1982 (Ps 51:16-17). Nashville: Thomas Nelson

[39] The New King James Version. 1996, c1982 (Ps 51:18-19). Nashville: Thomas Nelson

[40] The New King James Version. 1996, c1982 (Isa 32:16-20). Nashville: Thomas Nelson

[41] The New King James Version. 1996, c1982 (Jn 14:27). Nashville: Thomas Nelson

[42] The New King James Version. 1996, c1982 (Rom 8:38-39). Nashville: Thomas Nelson

[43] Nee, Watchman, (1972). *Spiritual Authority*. U.S.A.: Christian Fellowship Publishers Inc.

[44] The New King James Version. 1996, c1982 (1 Pet 2:13-17). Nashville: Thomas Nelson

[45] The New King James Version. 1996, c1982 (Prov 1:5). Nashville: Thomas Nelson

[46] The New King James Version. 1996, c1982 (Prov 11:2). Nashville: Thomas Nelson

[47] The New King James Version. 1996, c1982 (Prov 11:20-21). Nashville: Thomas Nelson

[48] The New King James Version. 1996, c1982 (Hos. 6:6). Nashville: Thomas Nelson

[49] *Smith's Bible Dictionary*. (1962), Nashville: Thomas Nelson

[50] The New King James Version. 1996, c1982 (Heb 12:15). Nashville: Thomas Nelson

[51] The New King James Version. 1996, c1982 (Acts 8:23). Nashville: Thomas Nelson

[52] The New King James Version. 1996, c1982 (Eph 4:31). Nashville: Thomas Nelson

[53] The New King James Version. 1996, c1982 (Heb 12:14-15). Nashville: Thomas Nelson

[54] The New King James Version. 1996, c1982 (Psa 43:5). Nashville: Thomas Nelson

[55] The New King James Version. 1996, c1982 (1 Sam 30:6). Nashville: Thomas Nelson

[56] Marshall, C. (1982) *The Prayers of Peter Marshall* Grand Rpaids, Mt Chosen Books, a division of Baker Book House Co

[57] MacDonald, W,. & Farstad, A. (1997; c1995). *Believer's Bible Commentary : O;d and New Testaments* (Col 3:8). Nashville: Thomas Nelson

[58] The New King James Version. 1996, c1982 (Prov 16:32). Nashville: Thomas Nelson

[59] The New King James Version. 1996, c1982 (Prov 22:24-25). Nashville: Thomas Nelson

[60] The New King James Version. 1996, c1982 (Jon 3:10-4:1). Nashville: Thomas Nelson

[61] The New King James Version. 1996, c1982 (Jon 4:9-11). Nashville: Thomas Nelson

[62] Wiersbe, W.W. (1997, c1991) *With the word bible commentary* (2 Co 1:1). Nash-

[63] Hayford, J.W., Howse, G. & Posey, M. (1997, c1996) *Race and Reconciliation : Healing the Wounds, Winning the Harvest*. Spirit-filled Life Kingdom Dynamic Study Guides. Nashville: Thomas Nelson

[64] The New King James Version. 1996, c1982 (Isa 43:18-19). Nashville: Thomas Nelson

[65] The New King James Version. 1996, c1982 (2 Cor 4:8-9). Nashville: Thomas Nelson

[66] The New King James Version. 1996, c1982 (Isa 64:6). Nashville: Thomas Nelson

[67] The New King James Version. 1996, c1982 (Prov 30:12). Nashville: Thomas Nelson

[68] The New King James Version. 1996, c1982 (Gal 3:16). Nashville: Thomas Nelson

[69] The New King James Version. 1996, c1982 (1 Jn 3:10). Nashville: Thomas Nelson

[70] The New King James Version. 1996, c1982 (Prov 21:2). Nashville: Thomas Nelson

[71] Morgan, R. J. (2000). *Nelson's complete book of stories, illustrations, and quotes* (electronic ed.)(635). Nashville: Thomas Nelsom Publishers.

[72] The New King James Version. 1996, c1982 (Ex 23:3). Nashville: Thomas Nelson

[73] The New King James Version. 1996, c1982 (Deut 1:17). Nashville: Thomas Nelson

[74] The New King James Version. 1996, c1982 (Job 13:10). Nashville: Thomas Nelson

[75] The New King James Version. 1996, c1982 (Jam 2:8-9). Nashville: Thomas Nelson

[76] The New King James Version. 1996, c1982 (Heb 10:11-14). Nashville: Thomas Nelson

[77] The New King James Version. 1996, c1982 (Heb 10:14). Nashville: Thomas Nelson

[78] The New King James Version. 1996, c1982 (Gal 5:19-21). Nashville: Thomas Nelson

[79] The New King James Version. 1996, c1982 (Rom 8:1). Nashville: Thomas Nelson

[80] The New King James Version. 1996, c1982 (Heb 12:1-6). Nashville: Thomas Nelson

[81] The New King James Version. 1996, c1982 (Eph 4:22-24). Nashville: Thomas Nelson

[82] The New King James Version. 1996, c1982 (Heb 10:26-27). Nashville: Thomas Nelson

[83] The New King James Version. 1996, c1982 (Heb 10:29). Nashville: Thomas Nelson

[84] The New King James Version. 1996, c1982 (Heb 2:11). Nashville: Thomas Nelson

[85] The New King James Version. 1996, c1982 (Rom 6:1-2). Nashville: Thomas Nelson

[86] The New King James Version. 1996, c1982 (Rom 6:15). Nashville: Thomas Nelson

[87] The New King James Version. 1996, c1982 (Zec 3:1-5). Nashville: Thomas Nelson

[88] Hurley, V. (2000, c1995). *Speaker's sourcebook of new illustrations* (Electronic Ed) (27). Dallas: Word Publishers

[89] The New King James Version. 1996, c1982 (Gen 4:4-5). Nashville: Thomas Nelson

[90] The New King James Version. 1996, c1982 (Isa 55:8). Nashville: Thomas Nelson

[91] The New King James Version. 1996, c1982 (Eze 36:26-27). Nashville: Thomas Nelson

[92] Green, K. (1992). *A Cry in the Wilderness.* Sparrow Corporation: USA.

[93] The New King James Version. 1996, c1982 (Ruth 1:16-17). Nashville: Thomas Nelson

[94] The New King James Version. 1996, c1982 (Isa 42:1-9). Nashville: Thomas Nelson

[95] The New King James Version. 1996, c1982 (Isa 49:1-9). Nashville: Thomas Nelson

[96] The New King James Version. 1996, c1982 (Isa 50:4-11). Nashville: Thomas Nelson

[97] The New King James Version. 1996, c1982 (Isa 52:13-53:12). Nashville: Thomas Nelson

[98] The New King James Version. 1996, c1982 (Lk 1:38). Nashville: Thomas Nelson

[99] Hayford, J. W., & Thomas Nelson Publishers. (1995). *Hayford's Bible handbook.* Nashville: Thomas Nelson Publishers

[100] The New King James Version. 1996, c1982 (Col 1:3-8). Nashville: Thomas

[101] The New King James Version. 1996, c1982 (Col 4:12). Nashville: Thomas Nelson

[102] The New King James Version. 1996, c1982 (Phil 23-24). Nashville: Thomas Nelson

[103] Vine, W. (1997, c1996). *Collected writings of W. E. Vine.* Nashville: Thomas Nelson

[104] Hayford, J. W., & Van Cleave, N. (1997, c1993). *God's Way to Wholeness : Divine Healing by the Power of the Holy Spirit Life.* Kingdom Dynamics Study Guides. Nashville: Thomas Nelson.

[105] The New King James Version. 1996, c1982 (1 Pe 2:13-16). Nashville: Thomas Nelson

[106] Hayford, J.W., & Hagan, K.A. (1997). *Passing Faith's Tests with Love and Joy : A study of James,* (1&2 Peter, 1-3 John, Jude). Spirit-Filled Life Bible Discovery Guides. Nashville: Thomas Nelson

[107] Wardle, Terry. (1973) *Exalt Him.* U.S.A.: Christian Publications

[108] Hayford, J. W., & MacDonald, D.T, (1997, c1994). *Towards More Glorious Praise : Power Principles for Faith-Filled People.* Spirit-filled Life Kingdom Dynamics Study Guides. Nashvile: Thomas Nelson

[109] Osei-Mensah, G. (1990) *Wanted: Servant Leaders.* Ghana: African Christian Press

[110] The New King James Version. 1996, c1982 (Jdg 17:6). Nashville: Thomas Nelson

[111] The New King James Version. 1996, c1982 (Mt 20:26-28). Nashville: Thomas Nelson

[112] Bailey, B. J., (2004) *Leadership.* U.S.A.: Zion Christian Publishers

[113] The New King James Version. 1996, c1982 (Heb 5:1-4). Nashville: Thomas Nelson

[114] Maxwell, John, C. (2000). *The 21 most powerful minutes in a leaders day.* U.S.A.: Thomas Nelson Publishers

[115] Maxwell, John. C., (1993). *Developing the leader within you.* U.S.A.: Injoy Inc.

[116] Leighton Ford,. *Transforming Leadership.* (Downer's Grove, IL: InterVarsity Press, 1991) 37-38

[117] Murphy, E.F. (1997, c1996). *Handbook for spiritual warfare.* Nashville: Thomas Nelson.

[118] Witherington III, Ben., *Conflict and Community in Corinth.* (Grand Rapids: Eerdmans, 1995)

[119] Hayford, J.W. & Snider, J. (1997, c1995) *Twelve Voices for Truth: Confronting a*

Fallen World with Hope: A study of the minor Prophets. Spirit-Filled Life Bible Discovery Guides. Nashville: Thomas Nelson

[120] Thomas Nelson, I. (1997, c1995). *Womens Study Bible.* (2 Ki 7:6). Nashville: Thomas Nelson

[121] http://www.leadershipnow.com/leadershipquotes.html

[122] Hayford, J.W., & Parrish, M.W. (1997, c1994). *Biblical ministries through women: God's daughters and God's work.* Spirit-Filled Life Kingdom Dynamics Study Guides. Nashville: Thomas Nelson

[123] The New King James Version. 1996, c1982 (Ez 34:1-10). Nashville: Thomas Nelson

[124] The New King James Version. 1996, c1982 (Jn 10:11-16). Nashville: Thomas Nelson

[125] The New King James Version. 1996, c1982 (Jn 21:15-19). Nashville: Thomas Nelson

[126] The New King James Version. 1996, c1982 (1 Pe 5:2-5). Nashville: Thomas Nelson

[127] The New King James Version. 1996, c1982 (1 Th 5:12-15). Nashville: Thomas Nelson

[128] The New King James Version. 1996, c1982 (Mt 7:12). Nashville: Thomas Nelson

[129] Hayford, J.W., & Snider, J. (1997, c1995). *Twelve Voices for Truth: confronting a Fallling World for Hope: A Study of the minor Prophets.* Spirit-Filled Life Bible Dictionary Guides. Nashville: Thomas Nelson.

[130] Hayford, J.W., & Snider, J. (1997, c1995). *Twelve Voices for Truth: confronting a Fallling World for Hope: A Study of the minor Prophets.* Spirit-Filled Life Bible Dictionary Guides. Nashville: Thomas Nelson.

[131] Thomas Nelson Publishers. (2001) *What does the Bible say about_ : The ultimate A to Z resource fully illustrated.* Nelson's A to Z series (Page 362). Nashville, ten.: Thomas Nelson

[132] Hayford, J.W., & Rosenberger, H. (1997, c1994) *Appointed to Leadership: God's Principles for Spiritual Leaders.* Spirit-filled Life Kingdom dynamic study guides. Nashville: Thomas Nelson.

[133] The New King James Version. 1996, c1982 (2 Cor 4:8-10). Nashville: Thomas Nelson

[134] Hayford, J.W. (1998). *Ministering in the Spirit and Strength of Jesus.* Nashville: Thomas Nelson

[135] MacDonald, W,. & Farstad, a. (1997, c1995) *Believers Bible Commentary: Old and New Testaments (Ro 12:15).* Nashville: Thomas Nelson

[136] The New King James Version. 1996, c1982 (Ro 12:15). Nashville: Thomas

[137] The New King James Version. 1996, c1982 (Prov 14:10). Nashville: Thomas Nelson

[138] Radmacher, E. D., Allen, R. B., & House, H. W., (1999). *Nelson's new illustrated bible commentary* (Pr 14:10). Nashville: Thomas Nelson

[139] Hayford, J.W., & Thomas Nelson Publishers. (1995). *Hayford's Bible Handbook.* Nashville: Thomas Nelson

[140] The New King James Version. 1996, c1982 (Job 2:11-13). Nashville: Thomas Nelson

[141] KJV Bible Commentary. (1997, c1994) (937). Nashville: Thomas Nelson

[142] Thomas Nelson Publishers. (2001). *What does the Bible say about - : The ultimate A to Z resource fully illustrated.* (123). Nashville Tenn.: Thomas Nelson

[143] Morgan, R.J. (2000). *Nelson's complete book of stories, illustrations, and quotes* (Electronic ed) (255). Nashville: Thomas Nelson

[144] Morgan, R.J. (2000). *Nelson's complete book of stories, illustrations, and quotes* (Electronic ed) (258). Nashville: Thomas Nelson

[145] Morgan, R.J. (2000). *Nelson's complete book of stories, illustrations, and quotes* (Electronic ed) (256). Nashville: Thomas Nelson

[146] Morgan, R.J. (2000). *Nelson's complete book of stories, illustrations, and quotes* (Electronic ed) (258). Nashville: Thomas Nelson

[147] The New King James Version. 1996, c1982 (Ex 18:21). Nashville: Thomas Nelson

[148] Thomas Nelson Publishers. (2001). *What does the Bible say about - : The ultimate A to Z resource fully illustrated.* (123). Nashville Tenn.: Thomas Nelson

[149] Youngblood, R.F., Bruce, F.F., Harrison, R.K., & Thomas Nelson Publishers. (1995). *Nelson's new illustrated Bible dictionary.* Rev. ed. of: Nelson's illustrated Bible dictionary.: Includes index. Nashville: T. Nelson

[150] The New King James Version. 1996, c1982 (Prov 4:25-27). Nashville: Thomas Nelson

[151] The New King James Version. 1996, c1982 (2 Cor 4:16-18). Nashville: Thomas Nelson

[152] Daniel, D. (2005). *Biblical Leadership.* R.S.A.: Creda Communications

[153] The New King James Version. 1996, c1982 (Ps 26:2). Nashville: Thomas Nelson

[154] The New King James Version. 1996, c1982 (1 Th 5:21). Nashville: Thomas Nelson

[155] The New King James Version. 1996, c1982 (Jer 30:2). Nashville: Thomas Nelson

[156] The New King James Version. 1996, c1982 (Hab 2:2-4). Nashville: Thomas Nelson

[157] Hayford, J.W., & Hayford. J.W.I., (1997, c1996) *Fearless Faith : Standing firm in the Freedom and Hope: A study of Galatians, 1 &2 Thessalonians.* Spirit-Filled Life Bible Discovery Guides. Nashville: Thomas Nelson

[158] Morgan, R.J., (2000, c1997) *On this day : 265 amazing and inspiring stories about saints, martys and heroes* (Electronic ed) (May 28) Nashville: Thomas Nelson

[159] Morgan, R.J., (2000, c1997) *On this day : 265 amazing and inspiring stories about saints, martys and heroes* (Electronic ed) (Jul 25) Nashville: Thomas Nelson

[160] The New King James Version. 1996, c1982 (Prov 29:18). Nashville: Thomas Nelson

[161] The New King James Version. 1996, c1982 (Hab 2:2-4). Nashville: Thomas Nelson

[162] Damazio, F. (1980). *The Making of a Leader.* U.S.A.: Bible Temple Inc

[163] The New King James Version. 1996, c1982 (Isa 53:12). Nashville: Thomas Nelson

[164] Hayford, J.W., & Thomas Nelson Publishers. (1995) *Hayford's Bible Handbook.* Nashville: Thomas Nelson Publishers

[165] Hayford, J.W., & Thomas Nelson Publishers. (1995) *Hayford's Bible Handbook.* Nashville: Thomas Nelson Publishers

[166] Hayford, J.W., & Thomas Nelson Publishers. (1995) *Hayford's Bible Handbook.* Nashville: Thomas Nelson Publishers

[167] The New King James Version. 1996, c1982 (1 Tim 2:1-4). Nashville: Thomas Nelson

[168] The New King James Version. 1996, c1982 (Eze. 22:30). Nashville: Thomas Nelson

[169] Hayford, J.W., & Hayford, M. (1997, c1993). *Kingdom warfare : prayer, spiritual warfare and the ministry of angels.* Spirit-Filled Life Kingdom Dynamics Study Guides. Nashville: Thomas Nelson

[170] The New King James Version. 1996, c1982 (Is. 58:12). Nashville: Thomas Nelson

[171] The New King James Version. 1996, c1982 (Rom 8:26-28). Nashville: Thomas Nelson

[172] The New King James Version. 1996, c1982 (Heb. 7:24-25). Nashville: Thomas Nelson

[173] Hayford, J.W., & Hayford, M. (1997, c1993). *Kingdom warfare : prayer, spiritual warfare and the ministry of angels.* Spirit-Filled Life Kingdom Dynamics Study Guides. Nashville: Thomas Nelson

[174] The New King James Version. 1996, c1982 (Rom 8:26-28). Nashville: Thomas Nelson

[175] The New King James Version. 1996, c1982 (Jn. 12:1-3). Nashville: Thomas Nelson

[176] McGee, J.V., (1997, c1981). *Thru the Bible commentary.* Baesed on the Thru the Bible radio programme. (Electronic ed) (4:450-451). Nashville: Thomas Nelson

[177] Richards, L., Pergoda, D., & Gross, P. (2001). *Every teaching of Jesus in the Bible.* Includes index. (Page 154). Nashville: T Nelson

[178] The New King James Version. 1996, c1982 (Neh. 1:1-11). Nashville: Thomas Nelson

[179] The New King James Version. 1996, c1982 (Neh. 2:4-6). Nashville: Thomas Nelson

[180] The New King James Version. 1996, c1982 (Neh. 2:17-20). Nashville: Thomas Nelson

[181] The New King James Version. 1996, c1982 (Neh. 4:7-8). Nashville: Thomas Nelson

[182] The New King James Version. 1996, c1982 (Neh. 5:1-13). Nashville: Thomas Nelson

[183] The New King James Version. 1996, c1982 (Num. 20:7-12). Nashville: Thomas Nelson

[184] The New King James Version. 1996, c1982 (Neh. 5:14-18). Nashville: Thomas Nelson

[185] The New King James Version. 1996, c1982 (Neh. 8:8). Nashville: Thomas Nelson

[186] Richards, L. (1999). *Every man in the Bible.* (143). Nashville: T. Nelson

[187] The New King James Version. 1996, c1982 (Mk. 16:14). Nashville: Thomas Nelson

www.ingramcontent.com/pod-product-compliance
Lightning Source LLC
LaVergne TN
LVHW051500070426
835507LV00022B/2864